My P:

Boxing Legend

Ken Buchanan MBE

15 Rounds of Great Memories with Ken Buchanan MBE, Scotland's
Greatest ever boxer. By, Jock Mcinnes MBE.
Front Cover and above Photo –Jock Mcinnes and
Ken Buchanan (Cyprus 2006)

My Pal, The Boxing Legend,
First edition August 2020

ISBN 9781838186807

Cover design and book layout by Tay IT.
https://tayit.co.uk

To my son, Stuart Mcinnes

Acknowledgements

I, Jock Mcinnes, wish to thank all my Family and friends (pals in Scotland), for their persistence, nudges, urgings and wee reminders to help turn my notes, comments and wee stories, into this gorgeous wee book.

In particular, I would like to thank my good lady, boss, partner and wife Christine, my mum Nancy (RIP), my dad Bill (RIP), Willie (Brother) and his life partner Arleen, Janet (BIG twin sis), Jim (brother in law), Kirsty & Bairns, oor Sean and his lass Amber, and not forgetting Lloyd or as I call him wee Jock.

Also, Stuart (my son), Moira and my lovely granddaughter Eilidh, grandson Callum, my very good pal Mick Scott, and not forgetting Colin Lamont aka Monty, for his time in editing the raw manuscript I produced, into this book, over a period of many months. And to everyone else that had some input into the thinking, writing and production of my book, my sincerest thanks to you all.

P.s. I will buy you a drink when I get my first million, Yeh right. Cheers.

Sponsors

I would like to thank the following friends of both Ken and I,
For kindly sponsoring this wee book.

PHOENIX ROADMARKINGS,
Expert Road Marking Services throughout
Scotland. Call Us On 07803838785

Greg & Margaret Keenan
"Proud to call both the author and the Legend friends" thanks for the
memories, Greg & Margaret Keenan, the Taybank group, `1984 – 2004

Phil Jones
Born and bred in Merthyr Tydfil, Wales
lifelong friend of Ken Buchanan MBE for over 55 years.
and big supporter of Jock and his charity work.

The Hughes Family
Norman, Thomas and Aidan from
Fair City ABC, all big supporters of
Ken Buchanan MBE and his pal Jock.

Jock Mcinnes MBE & Ken Buchanan MBE

Jock Mcinnes MBE Climbing Mt Elbrus for Charity

Contents

Contents

Contents

Contents

Introduction

"If you work hard in training, the fight is easy." -Manny Pacquiao

Introduction

It's pretty normal for a book today to have a lengthy introduction, in which the author explains the motivation behind the contents. But this is a wee book written by a wee man, no one special, and wherever you've borrowed, pinched or even bought this book, you really only want to do one thing eh, and that's read it. Lol, so pull up a seat, get yourself a nice cold beer and enjoy. Oh, but before you do let me finish this introduction lol.

Have you ever sat down and thought, I'll have to remember that? Well, I have on several occasions. Someone once said to me "Jock you could write a book on what you've seen and done" and they would be right, but as I said with a laugh on that occasion, "A good part of it would be unprintable."

However, having eventually gotten around to putting pen to paper, the book I have written is about a good honest friendship between two pals. One just happens to be the greatest pound for pound boxer that has ever come out of the UK and the other, me, a wee lad from the Kingdom of Fife. I spent most of my adult life, aye some of you will be thinking when did he grow up lol, in a proud Highland regiment which goes by the name of the first Battalion the Black Watch (BW), Royal Highland Regiment

1

Introduction

(RHR).

Why did I start to write down old stories about me and Ken Buchanan? Well, one of my heroes was the former boxing legend, Benny Lynch. Benjamin Lynch, to give him his full name, was born on 2 April 1913 and passed on 6 August 1946. He boxed in the flyweight division.

He is considered by some to be one of the finest boxers below the lightweight division in his era and has been described as the greatest fighter Scotland ever produced. On 21 August 1939, the Boxing Board refused his application for the restoration of his boxing license, stating that 'Mr Lynch is at present not fit to carry on a career as a professional boxer.' He turned to alcohol and would continue to battle with alcoholism for the rest of his life, despite several attempts to treat the disease. Lynch died in 1946 of malnutrition-induced respiratory failure, aged 33. He was buried at St.Kentigern's Cemetery, Glasgow, with some 2000 people attending the funeral.

There has been a couple of stage plays and documentary films, based on Lynch's life, but there are no records or stories about his day-to-day life and struggles, after the end of his professional boxing career. That is a shame because he had so many stories to tell, including his participation in boxing booth fights. He was a world champion none the less and he was inducted into the Ring Magazine Hall of Fame in 1986 and the International Boxing Hall of Fame in 1998. (Posthumously). I would love to have heard what he got up to on a daily bases, stories like his time spent in a sanatorium in Kent, and a monastery near Waterford, but alas that is now gone like the past.

So, I decided to write about me and Ken. Stories about our friendship, our excursions, our journey through life, not as boxers but as two good

Introduction

pals. Memories are like photographs, once captured they remind you of times that are gone forever. These memories are my photographs. Enjoy.

Ken Buchanan, MBE, was born In Edinburgh on 28-06-1945 and is widely considered the greatest boxer Scotland has ever produced and one of the very best from Britain. Ken was born and raised in Edinburgh, where his family lived in a modest council house.

Ken has always said he would have won nothing without his dad's support. Tommy, Kens dad, was at his son's side every moment of the journey, which saw him become arguably Scotland's greatest ever boxer. Tommy passed on at the age of 97, on the 7th July 2012 and Kens mum Cathy died of cancer, aged 51 in 1968. Ken often said, "I'm lucky because I had a great father and a great mother, so I have nothing to complain about."

My own father, Bill, was a very good amateur boxer in his day and also served in the Army, like me, in the Black watch. He had boxed Ken as an amateur twice, but sorry to say he lost on both occasions. Ken always used to say he had some hard fights with my dad and he presented me with an original boxing poster from one of the bouts, which I still have to this day. He also gave me an amateur boxing record card with my dad's name on it, which is now framed and hangs on my wall. My mum, Nancy, worked alongside Kens mum, Cathy, in Woolworths shop as a cleaner, so yes, our family ties go way back.

'He's a legend.' Back in the day that phrase used to mean something, reserved only for the special few that truly earned the status. Nowadays, it feels like it's thrown around to anyone. Apparently, there are legends everywhere. The title of 'legend' has become devalued. It has become overused and it has become confused. There's not one clear definition of a 'legend,' there are many, most of which are subjective.

As sports and boxing fans, we often sit down with our friends with a beer in hand and pose the question, 'Who is a boxing legend?' Now this is a bugger of a question to answer and the answer may vary from person to person and generation to generation, due to age, sporting prowess and bias, so coming to a precise conclusion is a massive task. It is a common fact, which most of us will deny, that we tend to favour a person of our own nation, but being a proud scot, in boxing, you can't go wrong. Scotland has been blessed with many world class boxers including, Benny lynch, Dick Mctaggart, Jim Watt, and even today Josh Taylor. History will tell if young Josh can take the mantle of the true legend, but for me Ken Buchanan tops the lot. A true Legend, that's Ken.

I have written this wee book in the order that stories and events came to mind, so it's not all in chronological order. However, that does not detract from the flow of the information and the genuine laughter and banter that you will read about along the way. I have not written down every little thing we done together, or you would need a fork-lift truck to pick the book up, but I have written about selected great memories with the great man himself. So please read on and I hope you enjoy reading my stories and unforgettable memories, stories of real life and times in the company of a sporting Legend. Oh, and I make no apology for the bad language, cheers.

It is sad to say but Ken, (Ken Buchanan), like Glasgow's Benny Lynch, will be more famous when he is dead than whilst he is alive and with us today. Is that no a shame? No, it's disgusting and disrespectful for such an historically great world champion boxer.

Introduction

The people who make up the Edinburgh council, and those who sit in the Scottish parliament in Hollyrood, should all hang their heads in shame for not holding Ken aloft and parading him for all Scotland and the world to pay homage to. Rant over. I will climb down of my soap box and let you get on with reading this wee book.

Round 1

"The same hand that can write a beautiful poem, can knock you out with one punch—that's Poetic Justice." - "Irish" Wayne Kelly

First BW Novice Boxing Championships

It was whilst serving, in the years 1985-86, as an assistant physical training instructor at the Scottish infantry training depot Glencorse, just South of Edinburgh, that I first met Ken Buchanan (Ken). My own Regiment, the first Battalion the Black Watch (BW) (RHR), were stationed in the capital at Redford Barracks Edinburgh not that far from me. So, it was inevitable that I still popped along to see the boys at every opportunity. Around about this time, the regiment were in training for their company novice boxing championships.

I remember one of the lads saying that Ken had a pub down in Portobello and would it no be a good idea if he could come along on finals night, to present the trophies and speak to the young boxers. Agreeing that this was a great idea, I duly went to meet the legend taking along fellow instructor big Ricky Allsop, from the Kings Own Scottish Borderers (K.O.S.B's). We walked into the pub and I spoke to a lass behind the bar. "Hi hen is Ken in?" "Aye he is down in the cellar, is he expecting you?" she replied. "Aye" I lied, "I phoned earlier."

The lass pointed to the cellar door, which was open, so we both quickly popped down the steps. The cellar was dimly lit for some strange reason and it had a lot of electrical cables and stuff running across the floor and around the walls. There were numerous beer kegs attached to pipes running up to the bar above and a host of empties near the back door. At the far end sat Ken, doing what I assumed was paper-work, accounting and stuff.

"Hallo lads can I help yis?" "Aye we are from Glencorse Barracks, we phoned you last week about you attending our intercompany boxing championships up at the barracks and you said it would be nae bother. So, we have popped down to have a word about it." (Kens memory was never great). "Oh aye I did didn't aye" he replied in his Edinburgh accent. So, we arranged the details, a date and time etc. and happily left the pub. "Yir a wee lying bastard Mcinnes" my big companion said as we left. "Aye maybe so, but is that no a great result lol" I replied with a smile?

The night went extremely well, with the lads taking loads of photos and getting their hands-on Kens Lonsdale belt. I would like to think Ken enjoyed the boxing and the banter from the 'Jocks' and on his departure, he told me to keep in touch. I kept him to his word and phoned him a wee while later.

"How would you like to bring a team of your locals through to oor Corporals Mess for a Games night?" I asked. (A Corporal (CPL) is a junior non-commissioned officer in the Army) "Aye sure" he said. "Ok so why don't you come through and we will have a chat" I replied.

So, we arranged a date and Ken brought his young lady through to oor house and then on to the game's night. The games were even so it was time to throw in the Joker card. "Ken, how would you like a game of liquid draughts?" "Aye sure what's the rules" he replied. (Fuck this is going to be easy). I explained that the rules were the same as normal draughts, except you have nip glasses filled with wine and you must take (remove a piece from the board) if the opportunity arises? "Sounds easy" Ken said.

Aye yi are I thought to myself. I had sneakily popped a nip, (strong alcohol), into each glass containing red wine, but conveniently forgot to tell Ken as he had to drink it when he jumped me. Of course, he was winning easily but slowed down as the game progressed. The nips were kicking in and he was definitely slowing down and looking a bit green. "What the fuck is in this wine" he said. Too late the game was over. He had to go and be sick and forfeit the game, victory was mine. Don't play the game unless you have a very good chance of winning, I said to myself. Even to this day Ken brings up the time I almost poisoned him.

On occasion, I took young recruits to boxing shows to watch Kens stable boxers boxing at Livingston, telling the C.O. (Commanding Officer), that there will be no drinking on their part as the recruits are still in training. The N.C.O's, (Non-Commissioned Officers), will keep an eye on them I assured him. "Aye right Cpl Mcinnes" he said. He knows me well lol.

So, after a quick word to the young 'Jocks', reminding them that they are ambassadors for their regiments and not too let themselves or me doon, off we go. I told them they could have a fly pint but don't let me catch yis. How the hell does that work again? Break the rules but don't let me catch you? Yeh right ok, Lol. So, we get on to the bus at the end of the night and they are all pissed as newts. "Holy shit how the hell am I going to get this lot passed the guardroom" I remarked to the driver. "Nay bother" he said. (He was a member of my own regiment.) "I'll just no stop."

And that was the plan, pure madness but it was the plan. I got the jocks to put their heads down and their hands deep into their pockets to pay for the petrol, which of course went to the driver for taking the no holds route back to their quarters. Fuck me it worked a treat. The next day I was asked by the CO how the evening went. "Oh, fine just fine" I said with an impish grin. It was during this period that Ken had a book out, so I took the opportunity to sell some to all the young recruits. Ken took the time out to sign every book I put in front of him and he did them proud.

Making Contact again

I can't recall the date, but it was whilst reading a daily paper that I read about Ken and some incident in Coatbridge, between him and a woman. I immediately wanted to call him. I am not sure why, but I probably wanted to offer him some support and see how he was feeling. So, I phoned Ewan Graham, who had written an article for me regarding safety in boxing (but that's another story). Ewan knew Ken through the boxing circuit in Glasgow and gave me a contact number, gid lad. So, I give Ken a call and after around twenty minutes reacquainting ourselves with each other, we arranged to meet up and for Ken to stay the weekend in Scone, at my hoose.

Ken never had a car at the time, so I drove through in my wee mini metro to the Clyde football stadium, Broadwood, to collect him. He was dead on time, holding his overnight bag and dressed in a track suit and after picking him up, we headed north and talked non-stop all the way home. It was during this weekend that I invited Ken to our local lodge, Stormont, for a drink and I got Ken to sign an old boxing glove and present it to the lodge. During the night, whilst Ken was talking to a couple of the members, I spoke to the barman, an old BW pal called Sandy.

"If Ken comes to the bar to buy a drink don't take any money aff him, I will square you up later ok." "Aye sure nae bother Jock" replied Sandy. Sure enough, during the evening Ken gets up to buy everyone a drink, and as instructed Sandy told him his money is no good here. So, after Sandy explained himself Ken very politely said "Would you rather have a punch from me or Mcinnes?" lol. Ken spent some money that night.

Ken Recruiting for the Army

It was round about a date I am no quite sure off, when I asked Ken if he would do a wee bit for the Black Watch Recruiting team, with an old pal from the regiment, Ally Alcorn. "Yeh no problem" he said. I assured him he would off course get a couple of bob for the work. "You don't have to do that" he insisted, but I replied, "bloody right I do." I know the recruiting side of the military has a good few bob. So, it was arranged for both Ally, Mike Scott, who had never met Ken, and yours truly to go through to Kens house in a beautiful 4 x 4, which the recruiting team boss's ran about in. (I told you there was money in recruiting). We arrived at Kens in the morning and I introduced Mike to Ken, as he was to be Kens manager for the day. Mike was well made up and this was just the start of the three of us going out together. (Naw no like that ya sick bugger!)

We headed off to the Dundee home of Ally, where the recruiting team were setting up in the city square and Ally introduced us all to the recruiting officer. Ken went around and met all the boys in the recruiting team and had a good blether. I knew some of them from my serving days, Christ do I no sound old? Mike held on to Kens boxing belts to make sure they didn't disappear. Ally and the officer introduced Ken to the lord provost, who came down from her office to meet the champ and we spent a couple of hours on site. Ken had his photo taken for the local press and was happy with what he was asked to do. When the work was over, I said "let's have a well-deserved pint" and it was arranged for all of us, Ken, Mike, and myself to visit Ally's mothers house, for a wee Barbeque in their back garden.

The weather was unbelievably good for a barbeque which is unusual for this part of the world. That means it wissnae raining lol. We all settled down to enjoy the hospitality, food, and the crack, which was exactly as I would have expected from Ally, having known him for a good number of years. Ken as usual was in great form, recalling many of his boxing stories to everyone. A camera was produced, photos were taken and more of Ally's family joined in. The beer was going down very well, so we stayed for another couple of hours, after which we headed to Ally's old local pub. The folk in the boozer were amazed that the champ was in their wee pub and more photos were taken. More drink was consumed, and did I mention more drink was consumed? (Bit of a boozy story this is it no?)

These were real genuine people, hard-working lads who liked a wee drink after a day's honest hard graft. When we eventually left, the whole pub stood up and clapped Ken out the door and we got back in the 4 x 4 and headed back to Ally's flat in Perth, for a wee refreshment. Ally is good on the guitar and Ken likes to sing, as does Mike, and I like to assist where I can, so we had our self's a wee sing song. Boy were we no shit, but it was great fun.

World Boxing Hall of Fame 2000

I can't recall what the date or time was when Ken phoned but I could hear it in his voice that something was afoot. You never know if it is going to be good news or bad news, but this was neither, this was excellent news. Through an emotional voice he said "Jock, I have just had America on the phone, and they have said I am to be inducted into the World Boxing Hall of Fame (WBHF) in Canastota, New York." I was so happy and proud of my pal the champ. He sat and went through all the details over the phone to me.

The next day I rang Ally Alcorn, who in turn phoned another old BW pal, Davie Smith, a Piper. He asked if Davie would Pipe Ken onto the plane to start his journey to America in style. "Yip it would be an honour" he said and in fact the photo of both Ally and Davie is in Kens book, his autobiography 'The Tartan legend'. Davie adopted the mantle of Kens Piper and both him and Ally went through to meet Ken at the airport. Unfortunately, I had to work that day, as Ken was on his way to represent oor wee country in America yet again, something he has done many times before. Honoured in America and not a second glance on the streets of his native Scotland. Shocking.

On his return to Scotland Ken phoned me to tell me all about it. I have seen the video which recorded the great event and its braw. He was very excited and so he should have been, the first living Scotsman to be inducted into the WBHF. Benny Lynch was the first, but he got in Posthumously. What a great honour. He brought me back a WBHF watch and a WBHF baseball cap for my son Stuart, neither of which have ever left the house. Much later on in the year he would show me the video of the whole trip. He had been accompanied by two reporters, who sent back reports for their newspaper, The Daily Record, which gave Ken some very good coverage. Famous at last lol.

Testimonial Dinner

Ken invited both me and Ally Alcorn to attend his testimonial dinner in the thistle hotel in Glasgow, as his guests, and to say we were over the moon would be an understatement. We travelled through to Glasgow by train and were put up at one of Ally's army pals, in a house somewhere in Glasgow. A good lad, he even let us have the use of his driver to show us around and he dropped us off for a pint in the big city.

Much later that day the driver took us to the Thistle Hotel for the evening's entertainment. We were both dressed in kilts and were really looking to have a great night. We were not to be disappointed. We met Kens son, Mark, for the first time, a very nice polite lad, resembling his dad but better looking. He said his dad was away for a haircut and would not be too long. We had arrived in time to watch Ken, in his full highland dress, being interviewed in the foyer by Chick Young on TV. He was in full flow but gave a wee smile as, from the corner of his eye, he saw me lift ma kilt. Straight after this he introduced me and Ally to Phil, his Welsh brother. "Come on I will let you see around the place" Ken said. He told us how much he was looking forward to the evening and asked if we had accommodation for the night? Great.

Ken said he had given Phil, and his pal Mark his own bed as they would be sleeping in Cumbernauld. Shit, during our we stop off at the hotel earlier me and Ally gave both beds a "Frenchie"? (It's when you fold the sheets in such a way that when you climb in to the bed, most probably with a we drink in you, you can't straighten your legs and end up sleeping with yir knees round yir ears). Remembering that we thought

14

Testimonial Dinner

Ken and Mark were getting that room lol. Oh well, that's life I thought to myself.

We all trooped down to the bar reception for a wee drink before we got the call to take oor seats. We both sat at Kens guests table with Mark, Tom, Phil, and a few of his close pals, as Ken was introduced to a standing ovation. There would be an auction during the evening, for which I had donated a Spurs signed top, Hearts signed top, a large very expensive bottle of spirit, a Henrik Larsson signed pendant and a couple of other items, god I am so generous. We also did a heads and tails game at £10 per person. During the evening there was a man doing magic tricks, going from table to table and there were a lot of speakers.

A couple come to mind, especially John Gahagen ex-football player and John Conteh ex world light heavy weight champion. We in fact got oor photos taken with John Conteh that night and at the end of the evening, me and Ally got two minutes chat with Ken, thanking him for a lovely dinner. He was a happy man that night, but things would soon become sour. The organizers did not play fair with Ken, regarding payment, for what was in fact Kens testimonial night, but I will come to that soon. But the trip into the big city was braw.

Round 2

"I'll beat him so bad he'll need a shoehorn to
put his hat on."- Muhammad Ali

Military Burns Suppers January 25th 01

I was given an invitation from Ally Alcorn, including invites for my good
civvie mate Mike Scott and Ken, to attend a military Burns Super to be
held at the Territorial Army (T.A.) Centre in Dundee. Me and Mike had
to pay a nominal fee with Ken having a freebee ticket as usual. We got
picked up outside of the house in a mini-bus and did we no look braw
(We looked good). We were like shiny new pins, complete with bow ties,
when Ken said, "Do I have to do anything." "Eh no just enjoy yirself"
came my reply (a lie of course).

We arrived and were introduced to the senior non-commissioned
officer who was running the evening. Ken presented him with a nice print
of himself boxing to hang in their mess hall, as we took to our seats and
started on the meal. Mike thought this was a fantastic set up as he had
never been to anything like this before, but the best was yet to come, the
very, very late license. It was during this time Ken turned to me whilst
reading the evenings programme "Jock, who is this at the bottom, guest
speaker Mr. Buchanan?"

This was My cue to start back-peddling I thought. "Ken you always
said you wanted to get into public speaking, well treat this as your first

engagement." Boy, did he no go daft, you little shit, was the best complement he got out but still, when it came to standing up in front of all in attendance, he was great. His duck was broken at last. The night went well, albeit a slightly long drawn out affair for Ken and me, but Mike took in every piece of the evening (probably because he had just got himself a new bird). At the end of the meal, I helped Ken sell some of his books and he must have had a thousand photos taken. His belts were everywhere, with the lads loving his honesty and sense of humour. We stayed until about 6 in the morning and thought we had better let the bar staff go to their bed.

That was the first military burns supper we attended. We went again the following year, but this time we were picked up in Perth town centre at Greyfriars pub, as I had arranged for Ken to assist in the opening of the Greyfriars whisky cask. The Proprietor was an ex police constable from the Glasgow area and a good lad, so when he asked if Ken would be interested, I said I will see what I can do and we spent an hour in the pub with Ken having his photo taken etc. He signed a couple of bottles of their new whisky and was given a bottle for himself, which is another story in itself, but that will become much clearer later.

The bus arrived to take us to Dundee. On arrival, we got off and I introduced both Ken and Mike to an old regimental drinking pal, Duggie Graham. He was meant to be at the top table but Duggie being Duggie wanted to sit in oor company. He got his wish and again we had a great night. Just before dinner was served I excused myself and went off to the toilet, on my return I saw that the Haggis, Taties, and Neaps had arrived, so sitting down I started to get stuck in about it, but for some reason my dinner companions were in fits of laughter?

Shit, some bugger has drowned my meal in salt, but not letting on I carry on eating it. Thank Christ there was beer on the table I thought to myself. I soon realized that it was Duggie who was the culprit and revenge would have to be sought. It was after the meal Duggie stood up to give the Loyal toast, yahoo an opening for revenge has appeared. Borrowing a lighter, I put the flame to his arse. Brave laddie, he never flinched, even when his breeks were starting to smoulder and he had a strange expression on his face. When he was finished, he swore the place down. "If ye play wi fire you'll get burnt Duggie" I said, but it was all taken in good humour. We drunk till the wee hours in the morning and we all got off the bus in Scone waving it away, when Mike turned and addressed all who would listen. "Wait a minute I don't live in Scone anymore" he says. "Well there's nae taxis at this time of night but yir welcome to stay the night on my settee if you wish" I replied.

Aye yi cannie beat a good burns supper and it would not be our last together?

Court Case

I was asked by Ken to be a witness in court for him with his lawsuit against Mr. McLeod, one of the gentlemen that organised his testimonial dinner. Of course, I couldn't say no, so I duly left Perth nice and early and was surprised to find it was Kens dad, Thom, who opened the door for me at Kens flat in Greenfaulds. The expression on his face said it all. "He will no get up he's been on the drink Thom said." Shit this is all we need today of all days. Taking two steps at a time I entered his room to find him still in bed half dressed, with only hours to go until we were due in Glasgow. Glem, his land lady was distraught with worry. "Jock" she says, "he went oot last night with a couple of the lads, but all he was thinking about was those two buggers, Antonio and McLeod, then he got home and started on the whisky." That'll be the Whisky from Greyfriars I was speaking about earlier.

Ken was unceremoniously dragged out of his bed, shaken and then pointed in the direction of the shower. "Am fine the man said". "Aye you look it, now get a move on we have time to make up." Big Tam was going with us and he needed to be picked up on the way, so a taxi was duly phoned and off we went. We picked up big Tam, who was waiting in his best suit, a big laddie looking as hard as nails, and we stopped off to buy Ken two bottles of water because for some reason he was a bit dehydrated eh.

On arrival at the court we met up with Gerry, Kens agent, who looks not too chuffed. "Where have ye been" he complained. We were ushered into a wee room where we had to wait, whilst the judge took time to go over the case and ask a couple of questions to Ken. Kens dad shoved a coin into his hand to squeeze so that it would give him something to think about when he started to lose it. This took a wee bit of time of course, so we went for lunch in the court's café, where Tam told us Kens lawyer, Mr. McCann, was a great wee man who sat in a wheelchair. "He was once the top man in Glasgow, The Lord Provost, and we got on very well together as his father was an ex Regimental sergeant major (RSM) in the same regiment as my own in the war years" Tam said.

Mr McCann took no prisoners himself when it got down to court business, and even the judge new his place. Big Tam never got called up to speak, a good job because he would have scared the life oot of the judge. Tom, Kens dad, Gerry and I, all stood up and said our peace, which did the trick. Weeks later we were to find out that the hearing found fit to say Ken was due a lot of money from both McLeod and Antonio. It was just another great day in the life of oor Ken, but would he ever get the money?

Legend meets Legend 23rd March 2003

"What are you doing the weekend 23rd" Ken asked. "Probably taken in a match, what have you in mind?" "How about coming with me down to Newcastle to meet Duran (Roberto Duran)." Fuck me you could have knocked me down with a feather. It was as if he was asking me to go for a pint, not to meet his old nemeses from years ago. "Yir on pal, give me the dates and I will take a sickie. We will of course be wearing Jacobean dress (Scottish Highland Dress associated with the Jacobite uprising of 1745), well you have to look yir best in front of the media" I replied. So, the big day arrived, and I drove to Kens flat and aye, he was ready. "We will be taking my car" the man said. That's fine by me.

So, heading south we drove off with Ken driving as if he was wearing lead boots. "Slow down Ken or we will get stopped" cried this wee lad shit scared, speeding down the motorway. We chatted nonstop. "What are you going to say to Duran" I asked. "I'm not sure I might just smack him" Ken replied. Holy fuck this is going to be a meeting and a half I thought to myself as we turned off the motorway level with Newcastle. Ken drove until we got to a wee town where he decided it was time for a rest (I think he was referring to my nerves lol). We had a quick bite to eat then Ken drove to the out skirts of the wee village where he pulled over. He then jumped out of the car, came round to my side and instructed me to drive as he had to finish of his speech. Yeh right oh.

I soon found out why, the bloody roads into Newcastle were a nightmare and Ken admitted to me that he left the directions to our hotel

21

back in his flat, bloody great. So, on we drove then Ken told me to stop and ask a passing man for directions. "Where yi going bonny lads" the man asked in his broad Geordie accent. "It's a hotel by the bridge" Ken said. "Wae aye man, what bridge, and what side of the water is it on?" Oh, so there's no just one hotel then lol.

I drove doon a one-way street as a bus was heading towards us and Ken went daft. "Well you fucking drive then," I said. "Aye and that will be right" came the reply. Kens phone goes, its Phil Jones. "Hi lads where are yis?" Bloody good question I thought. "We will be with you in about 10 minutes" oor bold Ken replied, Yeh sure we will? After about 20 phone calls back and forth to Phil in the hotel we eventually arrived. "Are yis ready for a pint lads" came the broad welsh accent from the welsh brother, oor Phil, who has been a pal of Kens for thousands of years.

After throwing our kilt etc. into our room we headed off into the town centre to find our self a quiet boozer for a pint. Even before we left the foyer of the hotel, the boxing fans were gathering and booking into the for the night. Ken spent 10 minutes signing autographs etc. and posing for excited fans. We made our first stop, not at a pub which amazed me, but a sports shop where Phil bought a pair of boxing gloves, in the hope of getting Duran's autograph to take back to welsh valleys with him.

Ken wandered off to find a bank and after 10 minutes I say "Where the hell has he got to Phil?" Just then Phil's mobile goes off, its Ken. "Be with you in 2 minutes. I just had a phone call from Martin Devlin the promoter of tonight's show. Duran wants to meet me before the show tonight." Martin must be shitting himself we all thought.

The three of us piled into a taxi with Ken giving directions (now he knows where he is going, there's a first) and we arrive at a very posh looking hotel 5 minutes from our own. We pose before entering then, taking a big breath, we stroll in. I spot Duran at the far side of the hotel dressed in jogging bottoms, a wee t-shirt and a jacket. Next to him was a smart looking Panamanian chap and Devlin the promoter. They spot us entering and come to meet us. Duran hugs Ken like a long-lost brother and there are genuine tears in both boxers' eyes, (and here's me thinking Ken would kick him in the nuts). We are introduced and take a seat and Duran orders coffee. From that minute onwards the talk was all about how this meeting should have been arranged years ago.

I asked if it was ok to take photos. "No problem" the smart looking lad said. He was Duran's manager, Tony Gonzales, who turned out to be a fantastic character and who did everything in his power to ensure Duran was well looked after. Phil got his boxing gloves signed and he was ecstatic, and I got a good autograph for my pal Mike Scott, as I know how much he would have loved to have met this other legend. Still, I am here instead, yah bloody hoo. The two boxers exchanged small talk for about an hour before Duran had to go for a wee sleep before to night's meeting.

We said oor goodbyes and climbed into a taxi to head off to get our self's ready. "Hey what about that pint lads?" I ask. They both looked as if to say tough luck Jock maybe next time. Phil went to his room, me and Ken went to ours, the three of us happy with our wee unscheduled meeting. I thought Duran looked humbled, but anyway we got into our Jacobean kit and inspected each other, we were after all ambassadors for our country. Phil knocked on oor door and said we looked smart, there's no fooling oor welsh pal eh. He took a photo and we headed down to meet the promoter. He ushered us to a waiting room where we had a beer at long last, and were introduced to the announcer and the night's comedian and a couple of press lads.

We were led downstairs, to the awaiting attendance. Ken was Introduced to the awaiting crowd and me and Phil were privileged to sit beside him at the top table, as he was given a wonderful reception. Ken took the mic and spoke about him and Duran and what the meeting meant to him personally. He spoke from the heart, luckily Phil had it all on video camera, and after a while Duran was announced and like Ken, entered to a great reception. He strolled up to the top table, shook my hand, pointed to Ken and they both hugged each other for a good wee while and shed a tear each. A very emotional moment and one the boxing world has waited 30 years for. With the assistance of Duran's manager, Tony Gonzales, Duran spoke about what this meeting with his old foe meant to him. With tears in his eyes, he spoke about the bout which took place 30 years ago and his low blow, and how he respected Ken 100 per cent. "Ken was a great man and a proud Scotsman, " he said.

Yir no wrong their big man I thought. They both spoke to the audience for at least 2 hours before they, me and Phil went back up to the wee room. We were first in so that the fans could get a photo taken with the two legends and if possible, get a signature (They would but it would cost them). Me and Phil were in the privileged position of having both legends together for half an hour before the masses would line up behind some really big security lads, while Phil carried on taken the video evidence.

Again, for some strange reason the kilt was up around my ears when they both looked bored and they had a good laugh for some strange reason. I thought Duran was going to piss himself. A couple of hours later, the last punter left, and we sat and had a blether with Duran and Tony. At one-point Duran phoned home to Panama to speak to his family and Ken had a quick word just to say hallo etc. When did he learn the lingo, I thought to myself? I trooped off to get my beloved East Fife F.C. scarf, to get a photo of us all with me wearing it in the company of the two great legends. Duran had other plans and put the scarf on himself, ya dancer I thought, a good one for the home programme back in Methil"

In fact, he wanted to keep it. Why I thought, the sun is splitting the trees over in panama and here he wants a football scarf, and not to be left out Tony got my other scarf, the Proud to be a Scotsman one. He was full of thanks and invited us all back to his suite for a wee refreshment, yir on.

His suite was on the top floor and was just something to be seen. Duran spoke about how he was ripped off by his own manager before all his big fights with Leonard, Haggler etc. all through Tony his interpreter. We all put our two pence worth in and then Tony asked if we all wanted something to eat. "Naw but a drink would be nice" I said. "Aye, me to" said my new Welsh brother but just oor luck the bloody large fridge door was buggered or was it locked? Still who cares, we are in the best company you could get (but a wee beer would have been nice). So, we said our goodbyes with Duran inviting Ken over to Panama to visit his family.

Its back to our own hotel to see if a late drink was in order, no chance, last orders had been and gone hours ago. Fuck it, time for bed, and to think a wee man from Methil met the great Duran, fantastic time but I had now lost my precious scarf.

That man "Willie Pratt" 15th June 2002

My life time friend Willie Pratt, who has known my family for more years than I care to remember, phoned me to say that he is taking time out to pay his family a visit in Methilhill, Fife, for a weekend and would like to meet up with me to catch up on old times and any gossip. He was now staying down in England, in a place called Warminster. Great news pal. "Can I bring along a couple of good pals who would enjoy the crack?" "Aye of course wee man he said, yis would be staying over for the night I take it?" "Oh Aye." "Good, I will arrange accommodation." The weekend arrived and me, Mike and Ken arrived at Willies sisters house, nice and early. I had already said to him to keep off the drink until we arrived. He opened the door with his belly hanging over his shirt less body, jeez what a site, aye and he had had a beer or three. "Yir a shit" I said. "Aye ah ken" he says come in.

I introduced Ken to Helen and her man, Cliff, who were over the moon to have him stay the night. We had a beer and something to eat before heading off to the East Dock Bar in lower Methil, to watch the Irish play in the European cup. My big brother met us down there and we got a couple of seats, but Willie P and my brother decided to stand at the bar. The drink and banter were going down well when Willie P said, "Let's move up to the Douglas when this finishes." "Aye ok" we replied. My brother tapped a couple of pound off me and said he will meet up with us later, aye sure thing bro, and of to the Douglas we went.

The pub was quite empty, so we got ourselves a wee carry oot at the shop with Ken getting wine and cheese? Back to Helens for something to eat then back oot, but Willie P never made it out again because he was fucked (I had telt him no tae drink too early). So, me, Mike, Ken, Helen and her pal piled into a taxi and headed off to the brother in laws boozer, McPhail's. We settled down to a good couple of hours drinking with Ken signing whatever was put in front of him, nothing was too much bother and the locals were loving it.

Mike's new Girlfriend had driven over with her pal to pick him up, as he had to get back for a Christening the next day, and he was being dragged in two directions. Stay with us or go with his girlfriend, but his loins won in the end and he disappeared. We jumped into another taxi and headed up to Buckhaven to a pub run by one of Kens old boxing pals. He was over the moon when we walked in and the punters were all up to shake his hand and put whisky down in front of him, which I quickly took and handed to Helen who never refused, with a smile.

We must have spent about an hour in this wee Fife pub before deciding enough was enough and again got a taxi back to Helens (bloody taxi service must have made a few bob of us this week end?) Ken kept asking where is oor hotel? Aye right. "Ok, I'll take you tae yer hotel Ken" I said as we walked through Helens front door. "Here's yir Hotel and here's yir bed" as I pointed to Helens front room and the settee. "Oh, ok he says," and we sat down laughing over a couple more drinks.

We rolled about the floor toy fighting which amused all. Ken was lucky as he eventually got the air bed and a blanket. I got the settee and no blanket, but it did not matter as I was too full of the amber nectar to be bothered about it. The next morning, we had a great breakfast. Ken handed over one of his autobiography's and a t-shirt from the World boxing hall of fame. Some of Helens relations came round to meet Ken and we left after about an hour heading back to Perth. Ken said he could do with a beer when we got into Perth. "Yip ok, lets park up and let's find out where Mike is." A quick phone call found him still at the christening just over the first bridge. "Come on over and meet some friends" he said, so we did and carried on the motion of enjoying oor selves. The poor wife was really pissed off, ach that's life.

Glenrothes shows 29th November 2002

We had a couple of trips into the Kingdom of Fife, Glenrothes to be exact, where I accompanied Ken to the Ciswo club. It was not confirmed by Ken why we were actually here, but it turned out to be an afternoons sportsman lunch. Ken took his seat at the top table alongside Kevin Drinkell (ex-Rangers, footballer and an international snooker judge). I was asked if I wanted to sit beside Ken but declined the offer, as I felt it should only be speakers and committee members who should have that honour.

The first speaker up was the judge who in fact was not bad and a bit of a comedian, then it was 'Drinks' turn. A right English speaking lad who enjoyed his fags, and again not bad but he likes to swear and tell old dressing room jokes, then it was dinner. The three old lads I sat next to, were a great laugh and very good company being typical Fifers, they said the speeches were not bad, but the next half of the lunch will be even better.

I take it they were referring to Ken standing up and doing his speech, wrong. Straight after the meal Ken got up and did his speech. He spoke very quietly but with a voice that said I have done it, no need to swear or make up story's, or make fun of his old foes and every ear in the place was his. When he finished, he got a great response from all in attendance and before the next part of the entertainment Ken took time to sign a couple of photos. This was my cue to pull out his books for sale and I started to sell the first 10 copies of his Autobiography, 'The tartan legend' but soon had to get the car keys of Ken and go and collect more. This happened at least 6 times with other speakers joining the queue to hand over their money for Kens book.

Ken must have sold about 40 plus books that day and several of his prints and as we all returned to our seats, a wee lassie walked onto the floor with a chair and her handbag. On went the music and she started to do her bit, yip a stripper. "This is more like it" said my fellow fifers sitting next to me. I looked up at Ken who just shirked his shoulders and laughed. At one point she made a point of dancing next to me and instructed me to smear baby lotion onto her back, as Ken was in fits of laughter.

We soon made our excuses, said our goodbyes and headed back to the car. I drove back to Scone, stopping at Duffy's on route for a quick pint. Ken then drove me back to the house then onto Cumbernauld as it was not too late. However, not before taking a cloth out of the boot and wiping both the steering wheel and gear stick. "I'm no having that stuff all over my hand" he said.

Round 3

"Everyone has a plan until they get punched
in the mouth."- Mike Tyson

Dusty passing away

Dusty was an older man who resided in the same house as Ken. He had
an illness from asbestos and was aware that he was terminally ill. He was
a kind sole who would do no one any harm and he was looked after by
Glem, who was like a land lady but treated all those that stayed under her
roof as Family. She would do anything for Dusty, Ken and John who all
stayed in the house and it was on boxing day that Glem phoned me to say
that Dusty had passed away. She took it bad. She said that she had paid
him a visit at the hospital on Christmas day to take him his present, and
he looked fine. She said, putting a brave face on it, that she would make
the funeral arrangements. (Dusty two sons were distant to their dad).
What could you say to her at this time? Ken phoned me not long after.

Ken also took this very bad, as he liked the old lad and he was very
upset. "Why could they no have left this poor wee man and took some of
those bastards, druggies, murders. There is not a God Jock, there can't
be" he said. Again, I was left without any words except to say, "Be strong
Ken, Dusty would have wanted it that way and he never suffered." Dusty
had left a lot of money to Glem who had nursed him in his last years, and
looked after his pals. She was in a panic about being left all this money,

so again my advice was don't panic. Dusty would not have left you the money if he didn't want you to keep it and worry yourself daft about it. The upshot is that wee Dusty had never told anyone, but he was still married. He never actually got a divorce and now his wife and two sons were fighting for the money. They were never there when their dad wanted them, or to look after him. There is no justice in this poor world really.

The Orkneys? 14th/16th January 2003

Now this is a good wee story. I sat at my computer one night and rattled of about six letters. Let's call them 'Kens potential bookings, letters.' The addresses ran from as near as Perth to as far as the Orkney Islands, with 4 of them going to Hearts supporter's clubs in Edinburgh. After about a month I thought that I would not get any replies when out of the blue I got a phone call. The wife shouts upstairs "Are you on that bloody commuter again?" Naw, I am windsurfing to America lol. "It's a Mr. McRae from the Orkneys." Aye sure it is tae. "Hi Bro, how are you?" I asked, thinking it's my big brother having a laugh, but no, sure enough, it was the lad I sent a letter to in the Orkney Hearts supporters club,

"Hi, I got your letter the other day and would like to know if you can arrange a wee trip for Ken to visit the Orkney Islands?" Sharp intake of breath. "Aye, I am sure we can arrange something." "How much will he take for the evening?" "£500" I replied. "Aye ok." "Ok, the travel expenses will have to be worked out, as does the accommodation in the Orkneys." I said. "I haven't done this sort of arrangement before," Duncan McRae admitted "but that's not a problem, I will assist at this end." So, we phoned each other on a regular basis, tying up sponsors for the Ferry and Hotel etc. I wrote out a programme and did a poster and sent everything up by E-Mail. Technology is a great thing is it no? I explained all my Orkney plans to Ken and of course Mike his Manager, who would have to travel with his man?

Yip a lad's 'Beano, (a lad's holiday).' I had been organizing this trip for months with our Northern cousin and it's looking very good, but a busy daily programme, however, the rewards would be worth it, I hope. On the Wednesday of the week before we are due to leave, I get a phone call from Duncan. "Jock, bad news. The venue, the British legion club, has been flooded out. I am working on another site, but it will not be easy as I need to accommodate a lot of people plus a bar and the Orkneys are not blessed with a lot of venues, which would suit both." Fuck me its falling apart just two days before we depart, don't panic, it's only a setback, our man from the North will sort it out, wrong. He could not find another venue at such short notice but there is no way I am going to give up a good weekend like this. I need to think. Time for a long soak in the bath, to recharge my batteries and after an hour in the bath it's time to hatch another plan.

"Hi Ken, its Jock, we have a wee set back with the Orkney trip" I go on to explain. "So, how's about us three travelling down to see your Welsh brother Phil for the weekend?" "Aye that would be good how are we going to get there?" "By car" I said. "It's easier to fly and no that dear" he said, "I'll make inquiry's on the internet." So, I leave him with it and give our other partner in crime a call. "Hi Mike, its Jock." I go through my tale again and also explain plan B and is he ok to fly down tae Wales. "Yeh no bother, I did it for about six months last year," he said. "Oh, aye you did yeh" I said with a wee smile to myself, yip he's up for it. Ken phones me back and explains the costing which I can't afford. "Don't you worry about it I will see you ok," He had already phoned Phil and he was up for it too. Plan B looks like it's under way, the three amigos are off to the Welsh Valleys for a weekend. So, I picked up Mike at about 5:30, he was ready and raring to go. We had a good, traffic free journey through to Kens and we arrived as Ken was putting his gear into his car. "Are yis fine lads?" "Yip, ready to go" we replied.

Mike scraped the ice of Kens back window, yes it was a cold morning, and we arrived early at Glasgow airport, checked in and went and had oor self a cup of coffee. Ken issued the tickets, game on. We boarded oor plane with me like a wee schoolboy on his first trip away from home. I don't know why I was so excited as I have travelled all over the world and at times on my own in some shit holes whilst hunting out adventure training sites for the troops. Malaysia. Brunei etc. but this was a wee bit different, this was me and two very good pals away for a weekend booze trip, yahoo.

We were no sooner settled down in our seats when the drinks trolley was making its way down the aisle. Ken settled for a bottle of wine as did Mike, very posh, and I had a wee bottle of beer, I thought I may as well start the way I intend to carry on. There will be no sleeping on this Journey I thought. (It was only about 8am). The trip only took about an hour and a wee bit and it was cold when we arrived in Cardiff. We collected our bags and headed out of departures and standing there, waiting was our Welsh brother Phil. "Hallo boyos" he said in his broad Welsh ascent. "Had a good trip?" We jumped into his car and headed for Merthyr Tydfil. He said we would stop on route to visit the Welsh sporting hall of fame and that it was not very far away. The sun joins us as we park the car and start looking around.

The Orkneys? 14th/16th January 2003

It is set in a beautiful castle type place and we get our photos taken in the area kept aside for Johnny Owen, the Merthyr Matchstick, a great boxer of his time. He was a real Welsh hero. We spent time looking around at a group of period houses, which were in a sort of wee village area, where we have a laugh with the Welsh guides. It was a very nice wee place, but we had to leave, and our next stop was in Merthyr itself, at a hotel by the name of the Bestifa, one Ken has stayed in before. We had one room, with one single bed and one double bed. First in at night gets the single bed I remarked to my two travelling companions to which they both agree, which is strange so there must be a plan a foot. We climb back into the car and head into town for something to eat and we had a nice wee meal in a Hotel in the centre of the town. During the meal I went to the bar and ordered another round for us all and decided to pay for the meal whilst I was up.

This never went down too well with the lads, but who cares, someone had to make a start, or we would be seen fighting over rounds and meals during the whole weekend. We then headed into the town to see the Johnny Owen memorial and the Howard Wilson Memorial and get our photo taken with them. Whilst we were in the town, we headed to a nice wee bar and sat for a couple of hours. Phil had to head home. He had to see to the wife and plus, he was driving, but said he would meet up with us later at the hotel for a meal, his treat this time. We had a good wee drink and made our own way back to the hotel to get changed for the evening meal. We decided on just going out casual as we were heading out to a Football club afterword's and would save our suits for the following night. We all met up at the hotel bar before heading through to

35

have a very large boozy meal, which was a great laugh and then hailed a taxi to the football club.

It was fairly quiet with just a wee karaoke going on. Phil and Ken were catching up as me and Mike hit the bar. We sat down and settled into a wee routine, talk, talk, talk, drink talk more drink. After about 3 hours, Phil says he is taking Ken up the road as he is tired. "Nae bother pal, if you don't mind, we will just stay another couple of hours and follow you back." Aye right oh, Mike is thinking.

Mike is chatting to this lassie, who was very friendly, a nice lass. I stood back and let him chat away, but could hear him say "Commitment, aye no bother, I'll come down and see you once a year?" Christ I about spilt my beer, cheeky bugger. We had had our fill, so time for home/hotel and yes you guessed it, when we got in the room, Ken was in the single bed. "Just me and you in the big bed honey" I said to Mike lol. Certainly not the person he was wanting in bed that's for sure lol

I was once asked, do the Welsh wales and Scots get along? I can confirm, Wales and Scotland get along very well, despite Scotland's hot-headed temper. Wales seem to be the only one who can calm their big brother down. They go out drinking on occasion, and both are known to visit England on random occasions, as well as Ireland. We had a great weekend, we had had oor fill and we couldn't look at a drink on the plane. Wales we love you, like a brother many thanks Phil.

Kinross show

On our second trip to the Kingdom of Fife show we headed to The Laurel Bank Hotel in Markinch. It was supposed to be a Scotland v England select tournament, but it turned out to be local lads from the Fife/Perth area, boxing against a club from the north east Newcastle area.

Kinross show

We arrived with plenty of time to spare and whilst we were on route just heading into Bridgend on the out skirts of Scone when I asked Ken if he had everything. "Aye sure, no wait I have forgotten to frame the print I said I would give for the presentation." Nothing changes, eh? "Nay problem" I said pull over the side of the road opposite Duffy's.

I ran into the bar and asked Ian if Kens print was still on the wall? Sure, enough it was there. I will bring it back later was my reply as I collected it and ran out and jumped into the car. "On we go big man." As Ken was driving us out, I said I would drive back, and we soon arrive at the event. Good. "Would you like a wee drink then" he asks? "Aye, make it an iron brew," and off he goes and returns with the drinks. He's on the red wine and the boxing started late which is pretty normal for these events.

The evening meal was very nice, and more drinks were consumed. The organisers of the show were looking for sponsors for each fight, so Ken asked me to find out how much it would be to sponsor a bout. It was about £10 to £50, it's up to the individual they said. So, Ken sponsored two bouts, one at the start and one in the second half after the interval for £20 each. He wanted to sponsor more bouts, but I said no as he was not getting much money for his attendance anyway and now, he was spending all the money he was getting for tonight's show on the promotion of the show.

Can amateur boxers, box with a full beard, now there's a question? Standards were slipping and even the length of the boxing shorts exceeded the official length, not how I remembered the sport, but I must be getting old. During the evening on one of my many journeys to the toilet, I noticed an atmosphere which didn't quit ring true.

Sure enough, two lads just behind Ken at the bar wanted to do a bit of boxing themselves. I leaned over and said to Ken to quickly stand up and follow me. "How whits up" he asked? We had just got out of the way before the two lads started to throw punches. In no time bodies were all over the shop. It would not be good press to see the former world champion in the middle of punch up at an amateur boxing show. "Cheers" he said as we took our seats again and the boxing re-commenced. We continued watching the bouts until the announcer said before the next bout, "Can you please give a warm welcome to our special guest this evening Ken Buchanan, ladies and gentlemen."

Up he goes to do his work. He takes four young boxers into the ring with him plus his belts and explains one by one how he earned them, draping each belt over a young excited lad's shoulder. They were over the moon. At one stage he even got me up to present trophies to the boxers after their bout as the sponsor. He must have arranged this during one of my trips to the toilet. Ken sold a couple of his books but would not take a penny for any photos. He would also spend a couple of minutes with each young boxer telling them how good they were and encouraging them to stick in. The journey home was full of laughs, aye, the man is good company.

Scots boxing hall of fame, 21st Sep 2002

The phone goes one evening. "Jock how about a night in the Hilton hotel Glasgow?" "Aye sure, what's the occasion" I asked? "It's the induction of me, Jim Watt, Dick Mctaggart and another into the Scottish boxing hall of fame" Ken replied. Great. "What's the date and what do ye have in mind." So, it's the twenty first of September and he rattles of all the details. The plan was for me to drive to Kens in the morning. Tom,

Kens dads was also at the flat and we have a blether. Me, Tom, Glem and Dusty drive to Coatbridge where we will be staying the night, whilst Ken and Mark, his son, will drive his car. Kens daughter will be arriving later in the evening. We arrive at the event and look for Ken, but we can't find him. So, we head for the Champaign reception to find Phil Jones and his good lady, who had arrived up from Wales for the weekend. What a nice couple they are.

I also meet, Charlie Sexton, former BW man who has risen to the dizzy heights as a director of the Scottish boxing hall of fame and find Ken, who is holding court along with Jim Watt and Dick Mctaggart, just beside the reception hall. "So, yis made it ok" he says" I nod and me and Charlie reacquaint old times places and things we have done together. A lot of photos are taken by me, and Ken asked us to join him whilst he showed his presence around at the different side shows, amateur boxing, collectors selling boxing memorabilia etc.

Glem and Dusty are up for a wee rest, so we find a café and Ken as usual buys for us all. During all this time a film crew from the BBC are shadowing Ken to do a programme on him at a later date. It was Charlie's task to introduce each of the inductees on to the stage and to ask them to make a wee speech, why he needed a microphone I'm buggered if I knew?

The lads from London turned up in a mini bus to lend their support, Charlie Magri, Alan Minter, Billy Walker, etc. and this went on for a wee while, then it was outside to have a ride on an open top tram around the grounds. Did I mention this was also the first time I had met Kens lass Gwen? At the start of the day Ken asked me to video everything for him. "Aye sure how does it work" I said. "Oh, I will show you." To date I am still waiting lol. The film crew took a good shot of Mark, Tom, and Ken away out in a sort of park area, and now time is beginning to march on. Most people are off to get ready for tonight's big show and after a good wee rest, Glem and dusty together with Tom called a taxi. "What are you wearing tonight" I asked Ken. "My black suit" came the reply. Oh shit, I realise that I have left it at the flat, so we headed out to Cumbernauld via the back road with time now really against us.

We steamed through all the roads, got the suit and headed back to the Hilton. Quickly up to our room and a quick change before heading downstairs to meet up with the London mob at the bar. They were all in good spirits, what a crew they were, full of mischief and fun as we shared the minibus to the Hilton. We arrived in plenty of time to meet up with Glem, Dusty, Tom and Mark and together with Ken and his good lady we headed in. Ken and his lady sat at the top table and part of the event was held in a very posh marquee with silver service waiters and waitresses, boy is this no grand I thought, I am going to make the most of this.

The drink was flowing like water, there was good banter and then the speeches start. Jim Watt gets up and says some really nice things about the day and about his old foe Ken. Ken stands up to reply. "What a lot of Shite you speak Jim" he says and the whole attendance are in fits of laughter. He can always seem to say the right things at the right times.

Everyone is enjoying themselves, then the dancing gets started and Tom is up of his seat and lets it all hang out with Kens lass. Down he goes, the oldest swinger in town. He is no sooner down then he is straight back up again, not bad for a lad of 86 plus. I forgot to mention it but Earnie Shavers, the hardest pound for pound puncher ever, is also in attendance and he is looking fit.

Scottish sports hall of fame

We go on into the small hours before the transport arrives to herd us all back to the Hotel. On our arrival Ken and his good lady say good night and head off up the stairs, which left only me with the London lads, what the hell, a pint of beer and a Bacardi please. I sit and blether with wee Charlie Magri and have a laugh with Alan Minter, who are taking the piss out of my accent, but I took it all in good fun, which is no like me especially from the old enemy. I used Charlie Magris phone to phone my sister Janet. "Hi hen it's me." "Ah ken it's you" she says. "You always phone me early morning when your drunk. are you enjoying yirsel?" "Of course," I reply. Would you like to speak to a couple of the lads?" "Eh no, its three o'clock in the morning and I am tired?" "Oh dear, night hen lol." (she still reminds to this day about the late phone calls, drunk, out with boxing legends lol).

Next day Ken me and his lass are sitting having Breakfast with the Cockney lads who looked dam fresh after having such a late night. It was during this time that Ken gets a phone call from his agent Gerry saying get a look at the Sunday papers. Kens other son had written a bad article about his dad, it was not good press. Today of all days. It should have been about his and others induction into the hall of fame, not this shit. Ken was going ballistic about this and he said his dad will be even worse. Not a happy ending to an otherwise great event.

Scottish sports hall of fame

It was whilst on the phone one night that Ken said he was again receiving another award, this time from Scotland. It's really amazing what people remember about a person once they have been honoured by others. "Yeh me and Jim Watt and Dick Mctaggart are to go to Edinburgh to be inducted into the Scottish sports hall of fame, then attend an evening function, it's going to be good, I am taking my dad along" he said. "That's great Ken, but not that I want to change any of your arrangements but don't forget you have a function in the lodge in Scone in the evening to go to. It's the one Frazer, one of my neighbour's, invited me and you to, your old pal Happy Howden will be there as the artist for the night" I replied.

"Oh shit, I forgot about it, right this is what I will do. I will go to the afternoons presentation then make my excuses and leave to attend Frazer's invite. I may be a wee bit late though." "Great" I said, "the lads are all looking forward to seeing you again."

I phoned Frazer and explain the situation to him, and he replied typically, "Oh that's ok I understand." On the evening of the event, about 6pm, I get a phone call from Ken. I am dreading it's not the "Jock I'll no be able to make it" pish, but no its Ken just looking for directions tae Scone. (He's only been coming through for a couple of years noo haha). He arrives with about two hours to go before we are due to be in the lodge and shows me his presentation. Its glass with a very nice inscription on it, superb. We have time, so we get the coat on as its cold out and head for the Wheel Inn just up from the lodge and only about two minutes walk. We have a wee blether and start heading down to the lodge. The weather is shit and Ken walks into a wee puddle right up past his ankles and into his socks.

"Oh, fuck look at me" he says, I'm noo in fits of laughter. "You meant that you we shit bringing us this way." "Aye ok Ken" I said getting oot of arm lengths way. We get into the lodge and right away Ken is off talking to someone. "I suppose I will have to get them in" I say to myself as no one else was listening.

We go upstairs and with luck I am sitting beside an old BW pal, Jimmy Melville. Sandy gets up on the stage and says a few words. "You may have noticed we have Brother Ken Buchanan again in our company and I and the rest of the lodge would like to say a big thank you for attending, as we realise that you were to attend an even bigger function this evening in respect of your induction into the Scottish sports hall of fame. Thank you for being here tonight."

Ken gets a standing ovation, so he gets up and presents his host Frazer with a nice framed print of himself, which I had put together for him about a week beforehand for him to ok and sign. It was another great night with Ken unusually running the raffle and auction, where a lot of money was raised for charity and a good time was had by all. The photo session at the end of the evening was a great laugh and we were last seen going arm in arm up the road singing. The wife even heard us whilst sitting in her pal's house as we went by.

Burns supper Guildtown February 2003

I have been looking forward to this wee Burns supper for a while, but it turned out to be remembered for all the wrong reasons. Ken phoned me both the evening before and in the morning of the function to ask when he had to be at my house. Knowing Kens sense of direction, I said be here for 2pm. "Yip no problem" he said and did he no amaze me by being on time (a first). So, at 2:15pm we went across the park to watch Mikes son, Brian, play for Scone Jnrs against Cupar Angus where we meet up with Mike. It was not a great game, but young Brian scored the only goal and as it was getting cold, we headed off in my car to see if Mikes sister in-law, Lesley, would give me a free haircut. We all marched into her house where I was duly informed that she had no shears in the house so that plan

43

wissnae happening, so but both Ken and Mike had a beer from Dave whilst I had a Coffee.

We blether for a while then headed down to Mikes to pick up his suit for the evening, with the next stop being the lodge at 5:30pm. We were getting picked up at the house at 7pm so time was on our side. The plan was, a quick pint and back to the house to get showered and changed before Tosh came to pick us up. It's 6:15pm and we are still having a drink in the lodge. "Right that's it, time to go" I said. "Bugger off" they said. "We have plenty of time" and up came a couple of beers which soon shut me up. At 6:40pm we are heading to the house. We were like the odd couple with everyone looking out for their self's, one in the shower, one shouting to get in and me, well I am panicking am I no. Up drives Tosh. "Yir best to come in and wait mate were running a wee bit late" says I. "Nay rush lads yi hae plenty time" he says. Good lad.

I was warned off that I will be up to do my poem that night. We pile into the motor after a good wee shouting match and we stroll into the local village pub as if we had all the time in the world. We meet people on their way out heading for the village hall and the supper but decide that we better have a pint since were here eh. Two drinks later and we saunter across to the hall, everyone is seated, and it looks like we are late again. We take too our table and start on the cans of beer on the table. Mike cracks open a bottle of Bacardi and Ken says, "I am no talking." "No yir no" I said, "they will just ask you one or two questions that's all." So, the time comes for Ken to stand up and make a presentation to the organisers. Does he no stand and speak for 20 minutes and receives a standing ovation, some man. He is presented with a very nice golf print and during his stand-up routine Mike passes around the Bacardi. I am up after the next speaker, so I head off to get changed. Things are getting a wee bit blurry now and after what seemed like an age I am told to head straight through that door and yir on.

Through I go, straight on to the stage. There are about 60 to 100 lads all looking up at me waiting for a real burns poem and I'm dressed like something out of the Bay City Rollers. Fuck this, I am no standing up here, so doon into the crowd I go and start doing my act, but for some reason all I want is a drink. It Must have been all that waiting, so I do my peace and head back to get changed, shit I am no feeling to good. Fuck me this is bad. I am never sick with the drink and noo I'm violently sick. I don't remember getting home or anything that night, it's certainly not what I had planned. The wife said Ken had to carry me up the stairs, and even had to take my trousers off. The next thing I remember its morning so, up shower and dressed for a walk in the park and to get the papers, hoping that would make me feel better but it didn't. I sit and read my papers as Ken strolls into the room. "Great night aye Jock?" he says. "Where's my belts?"

"Where Mike left them in the hall?" I reply. "How are you feeling to day" Ken asks? "Oh, brand new" I lied. Twenty minutes later we are sitting enjoying coffee trying to piece together the night's activities. "Did I speak?" he says. "Aye yi were no bad and you got a standing ovation." He was happy not to have let anyone down and I was just happy to be in one peace. Jimmy Melville, a good wee pal, phoned me up a couple of days later to fill in all the gaps and say that he had my camera. I now only have to locate my watch and I would be back to normal. Not like oor good pal Mike who told us later that he got us the taxi and shoved us in the house, then went to the dancing and got a lassies telephone number, what a guy. Ken drove off to meet up with his Welsh brother in Glasgow later on that night and he left the wife a nice bottle of champagne. (Creep).

The next day whilst having an Iron Bru in Duffy's, Ian the owner handed me Kens money for attending the Supper, £150. So, I phoned him up and said I would Send it on to him. "Nah you keep it, take the wife out for a meal or something." "No Ken its yours." "Nah I said keep it" Ken replied. So Fine. I did. I spent £50 on buying two tickets for him and me to attend East Fifes centenary Dinner, at the Dean park hotel in Kirkcaldy, on the 9th March and use the remainder of the money to keep us in drink for the evening, so he got it back again.

Duffy's Function Friday 30th Aug 2002

On one of my social visits to Duffy's pub in Bridgend, I asked Ian Duff the owner if he would be interested in running 'An evening with Ken Buchanan' some time. "Aye sure we can fix up a date and programme to suit" he said. I spoke with Ken who was up for it. Between me and Ian we fixed up a good fee for Ken. It would be a good wee function and of course oor pal Mike Scott would have to attend to keep an eye on the belts. The tickets would be sold for £10 each which was no bad. I put together a poster and made up a wee programme and asked Ken to bring through a good few of his books and prints. Ian did a good job organizing the press and Ken duly arrived on time again, (Christ he's getting good), and with Mike in hand we headed off to Duffy's. I off course had them in attendance far too early, still, we are in a pub, so we had a pint. Ken said not till later, fine we will have one on you then I thought. Ken, Ian and Bill Anderson from the Perth Railway boxing club (an old pal of both Kens and mine) got their photo taken for the local paper.

46

The punters soon started to pile into what was turning out to be a good night. Ken sat at the top table alongside Gordon Bannerman from the Perthshire Advertiser newspaper, who was acting as interviewer, and who I must say did a cracking job. About 70 people saw the tartan legend give a very good account of himself. Anyone who has heard Ken speak will tell you he speaks very softly and deliberately, as his family originally came from up in the Wick area of the north of Scotland. Ken, being brought up in the Capital, Edinburgh, where they tend to talk very fast, deliberately speaks slower when he does any public speaking. But yes, he did well, sold a lot of books and prints, and got his photo taken with a lot of his fans who all wanted to wear a world title belt. Ken me and Mike later sat and had one or two beers with the lads at the bar.

Round 4

"We may encounter many defeats but we must
not be defeated."- Maya Angelou

East Fife F.C. Centenary Dinner 09/03/03

I invited Ken to an East Fifes centenary dinner on the Sunday 9th March
2003 for two reasons, one was that I was on the centenary committee so
I had an obligation to attend, and the other was I was hoping Ken would
meet personalities to gain some after dinner work. I arranged for Ken to
be at our house in Scone for about 11:30am on the Sunday. As me and
the wife, Christine, sat and waited for him, she said "Well, how many
times do you think he will call asking directions then." "None" I said, "I
am confident he has got his sense of directions sorted."

No sooner had the words left my mouth, the phone goes. Christine
answers it. Its Ken, "I just turn right at the beef eater then a left, aye" he
says. Wrong pal, Christine has a wee laugh to herself. He turns up 10
minutes later, not shaven as he was running late, no change there then I
think to myself. We pack our suits etc. jump into Kens car, say goodbye
to Christine and head for my sister's house in Methil. I drive because I
know the way plus, I like driving his BMW. We make a short stop in
Lower Methil, at my uncle Charlie's and aunty Margaret's house for a
coffee and we stay long enough to make their day, mum will be chuffed.
We arrive at my sisters in time for a light meal and a glass of wine, game

on. The house is unusually full with my niece, Kirsty, having pals around who just happen to be big boxing fans. Brian, my niece's boyfriend's uncle, also popped round to meet Ken and have his photo taken. Everyone is in good spirits and Brian goes round to the wee shop for more liquid refreshments before dinner. Ken has white wine whilst I settle for bottled beer, this is braw. Janet nips out to get my mum who normally comes for Sunday lunch. My mum knew Kens mum as they worked together when she lived in Edinburgh. And lastly my big brother, Willie, phoned to ask when we were all coming down to McPhail's (Pub).

It was only 2:30pm and we had not planned to be at the pub for the minibus till 4:30pm. Willie had his girl, Arleen, and her family down to meet Ken. Ken was in good form, and we had more wine and beer before deciding it was time to get ready for the function. By this time, my sister had kindly re-ironed my suit which was covered in white fluff and my shirt which was white and fluffy lol. I got pelters for this from my sister, as she ironed Kens shirt and her man's breeks and in no time, we were all looking smart and ready for the off. We all piled into Janet's car, my mum also climbed in as we were going to drop her of at her wee But-n-Ben and we arrived down at McPhail's to find my brother in good spirits. He introduced Ken to all and sundry and I was amazed with Ken, he actually remembered Willie. I got the beers in again, (and to think some people say I am stingy).

We waited and chatted until the other bus passengers arrived and when they were all there, we went into the back room for a wee presentation. It was from those attending the dinner, to the gentleman who bought all their tickets and had arranged the transport, (Not ours). Ken was nominated to do the honours, so we drank up and drove west to Kirkcaldy. We spoke on the bus, but Ken looked tired. He asked about the tickets and who does he pay. So, I explained that I had got them which was a wrong move seeing as how proud he is. He wanted to pay his way saying that I had done enough for him in the past. "What you give a pal is no a loss" I said. "Fuck you" he says in reply, aye ok Ken.

We arrived at the Dean Park Hotel in Kirkcaldy and went straight to the bar, well it seemed like right the thing to do. Oh dear, £3 for a bottle of beer, this could turn out to be a dear night. We sat and talked before moving on to the free bar. Now there's a laugh, the bar was two tables set up in the walkway to a reception area. It would have been fine if you drunk Gin or whisky.

On passing the table with the Gin on it two lads were waiting for their drinks. "Fucking Gin," Ken turns to me and says in a loud voice. "only poofs and women drink Gin." I was in stitches; the two lads looked really pissed off, fuck them. Who was going to say anything eh? We entered the reception area where I left Ken talking to a couple of East Fife supporters whilst I went to find a bar to get a couple of bottles of beer. We only stayed there for about 20 minutes before taking our seats at a long leg of a table which was for the sponsors of the evening. I had to do some fast hands with the name tags, so that I was sitting next to Ken, but what I did not realize was that I had us both sitting facing Henry McLeish, the ex-first Minister for Scotland and ex East Fife player. After grace Ken got stuck right into Henry about not enough money going into sport for the Kiddies. "How did you ever get to be first man anyway" Ken asks lol.

Get in their Ken, he was on his soap box for sure. He was just settling down when he took a bite out of his roll, and in a voice that would have stopped buses he said, "Christ look Jock my tooth's fell oot." There he was holding his tooth and a roll. I can honestly say I have not laughed so much in all my puff, he could not get a decent word out of me for at least 5 minutes as he showed everyone his tooth. "I'll bloody knock that dentist oot" he says, still he had a good laugh (but no as much as me). I noticed there was no drink on the table. "Would you like a wee drink Ken?" "I'll have a beer" he says, but the lady sitting opposite me who was high up with the sponsors, Diagio's, said no we will get these gentlemen, (is she speaking to us?). Great then we will have a bottle of red and a bottle of white each? Ya dancer let's play I thought. We must have ordered about three off each for ourselves plus beer throughout the evening, as the night went on and on, but the meal was good, and the company warmed to us.

Ken was not off duty and still took time out to sign program's etc. After the meal and all the speeches were over, we got back on the bus. It was after midnight and we sang all the way back to Leven. One of the lads had a pub, The Brig Tavern in Methil, so we all headed for it. Sure enough, a rap on the side door and we are in. It was not empty and the beer was flowing well. Ken got behind the bar, pouring beer and getting his photo taken and still bloody signing things for anyone who wanted it. Me, Jimmy my brother-in-law, and Ken drunk until about 2am and decided it was time for bed or at least home. We ordered a taxi, said our goodbyes and swore we would be back, which I'm sure we will. We fell out the taxi, so my sister said, and she should know because she saw us oot the window. Jimmy and Ken were for some reason or another falling about in fits of laughter, one for the camera I thought.

On entering the house, we got the beer out, a bottle each, and spoke for a wee while before heading our separate ways. Ken upstairs to my nephews' room, Jim to his own bed and me, well I said, "I'm no sleeping with Ken or in that bloody Celtic decorated room." (which I have done before?). I woke up in the morning still in my shirt, tie and suit trousers with two wee boys sitting eating breakfast and laughing at me. I am sure they have been slapping my ears. "Bugger off" I said before heading into the bed they had previously climbed out of. We all seemed to get up at the same time. My sister was taking my mum to the doctors and said she would make breakfast on her return and true to her word she did, a bloody full cooked one too. I am going to struggle here I thought, and I did, Ken was no better, and he and Jimmy said they could do with a hair of the dog. Bloody dug must be bald by now I thought.

Willie, my bro, phoned to say if we were going out to give him a call, he must be psychic. Janet said she would drive, me, Jimmy and Ken, down into Leven on the pretext of me and Jimmy putting a spool into the chemists. I phoned my brother to say be ready we are on our way to pick him up. "That's braw" he says as he has library books to take back. (I found out three days later he left them behind a bar in Methil and got find £3). He was waiting at the top of his road dressed in his tracksuit as we arrived.

"Hi lads how are yis today." "Great how about you." Small talk till we reached the pub and a hair of the dug all round please, was ordered. I had a Shandy as someone had to drive us home eventually. Willie, my bro, was a wee bit skint but nae problem Willie, here's £10 to see you through the next ten minutes. The chemist was closed so they sat down and sunk about three each before jumping into Janet's car and headed to the East Dock Bar in Methil, a great wee pub where again I had Shandy, Ken, Jimmy and Willie were on the beer. After another couple Janet had to get back home for something to eat and we had to get our tales back home too. Ken had had too much to be able to drive back west, so we went back to Janet's to collect our kit and say our goodbyes. Janet said she will phone my wife Christine to say we were on our way back as Ken thanked everyone for a great weekend.

Ken left a signed autobiography and print for Janet and Jimmy, and said he would return, that I can believe. I took my time driving back to Perth with Ken who spoke for a wee while but drifted back and forward to sleep and at one point he shook my shoulder and said, "Jock if I ever come into big money were on for a big holiday together," somehow, I believed him. A real genuine guy.

We got in to the house on the Monday evening at about 4pm, where Ken had a quick cup of coffee before heading to his bed saying to wake him in an hour. I sat and had a lovely meal which the wife had made whilst Ken will get his in the microwave when he gets up the wife says. I sat and watched the TV. I was bored and was now looking for a hair of the dug myself so time to hatch a plan. I woke Ken at 8:30pm and he got up but confirmed that he could not drive back to Cumbernauld today. As he sat down at the table with a cup of coffee, I presented him with his meal, "Jock I don't really have this much for breakfast just a cup of tea and some toast will do pal?"

"Ken, do you know what time it is?" I said. Looking at his watch he says "Aye 8:30." "Aye very good Ken but it's no in the morning it's still Monday." "Oh" he says "what are we doing then?" "Follow my lead" I said, "just back me up." "Christine, me and Ken are popping out for an hour to take one of Kens books to one of the lads." Christine is obviously not happy is she. Ken pipes up, "We can take Christine with us, can we no?" "Aye yir right, I thought we couldn't?" Cheers Ken, thanks for the support, so, after a wee bit of a scurrile (comedy routine) we find ourselves heading into the town.

We sit in Duffy's and blether but to be honest all I was wanting was a hair of that bloody dug. We eventually went home in a taxi at 12pm as I was working in the morning. As for Ken, he had a long lie in, and just closed the door behind himself and put the key through the letter box, what a life.

Ken in Hospital (1)

After our weekend at the East Fife centenary dinner, Kens next appointment was at the Hilton in Edinburgh, at an amateur boxing show for one of his old Edinburgh buddies. It was to be on the Thursday night, 13th March 2003, and unusually I never heard from him that night. But on the Friday night I for some reason phoned his girls house, Gwen, to speak to him but, was informed that he was still in Edinburgh. She thinks he is on the drink, and yeh that's what I thought. She is panicking about his engagement on the Saturday at Banchory up by Stonehaven. She said his mobile is off and she can't get hold of him.

On the Saturday morning by chance I gave his mobile a wee phone. I get lucky and get him and say "Hi Ken how are you." "Oh, fine just having a wee drink with a couple of old pals in Edinburgh. "Good news, you sound happy, are you remembering about the Banchory engagement you have at 7pm today" I said. "Oh fuck, I will never make it." "You will if you get yourself on a train to Perth and I will drive you the rest of the way, you'll make it fine." "No, no I'm staying here for a pint" he said. "Can you no phone the venue and say I am ill or something, you think of something eh?" "Yeh ok I'll phone you back later. So, I did the deed and said he had a virus and was at his dads in Edinburgh laid up and would

55

not be able to make the show. I phone Ken back and tell him what I said. "Great wee man that will do." I thought nothing of it to be fair.

I get home from work on the Monday night, only for Glem to phone and say Ken was in Hospital. She never went into detail and said she would phone me after she had paid him a visit. During this time, I had arranged a wee paying trip for Ken and Gwen to a charity function in Edinburgh at the Hilton. It was a charity raffle, which I thought would be good for him and his girl to spend a night together in a posh Hotel.

Well I should not have bothered because when I phoned Gwen to explain what I had pencilled in for Ken, she was not too happy about me collecting Ken the day before. Nor for giving Ken bad advice about a character in Perth, who wanted to do some Business with him, a Mr. Rory Nichol, who we will hear more about later on. "Gwen, I would lie for Ken at a drop of a hat if I thought It would save him some grief and the business man in Perth, is good information I received from a very good source" I explained. It was in Kens interest to have whatever facts were at hand so that he could make up his own mind.

"I might be a little naive in my thinking but it's just my way" she said. Come into the real world one day Gwen, ours. Any way the next day Glem phoned to say Ken was fine and he was looking grand. On the Thursday, Ken phoned me from his girls to say hi and did I get my ear bent from Gwen. Yeh cheers pal. He said he had a lot of new engagements coming up, i.e. doing a TV broadcast for the Scott Harrison fight and talking at Stoke-on-Trent. It made my wee job in Edinburgh seem very insignificant, but he said he would go. Oh, I almost forgot, he said he was off the drink. He said that before he went to America to be inducted into the world Boxing hall of fame but that lasted for about 3 months, how long will this one last? For a very long time, I hope. It was about this time that I read in our local paper, The Courier, about a Glenrothes man who was going to raffle of a boxing glove which was signed by Ali, Lewis, etc. for the Multiple Sclerosis charity

Just to digress slightly, After Ken won the world title beating Laguna, he was again scheduled to fight at Madison Square Gardens in December of 1970 and was top of the bill. Muhammad Ali was on the undercard, having his second fight after his three-year ban. Well, Ali did not have a dressing room and Angelo Dundee asked Ken if Ali could share his dressing room. Ken, the gentleman, said "No problem." Ken walked into the dressing room and with a piece of chalk drew a long line on the floor. He turned to Ali and said "You stay that side of the line. If you cross the line into my side you will get this" and he raised his right fist up. Ali looked Ken in the eye, then they both burst out into fits of laughter. What a man.

So, back to the Glenrothes man. His name was Allan Noble. He ran the Snooty Fox pub on the outskirts of Glenrothes, so I gave him a call to ask if he had an auctioneer for the evening? "Yes" he said, "we will be using the chairman of the charity, it will be held in the 'Sheridan Grand hotel' in Edinburgh and was a big annual event, why was I asking." So, I explained that I was asking on behalf of Ken Buchanan who could have possibly done the job as auctioneer for you. "It would be great if you could arrange for Ken to come along and show his face," he said. I said I would speak to the man himself and we spoke briefly about expenses etc.

After speaking with Ken, he said he would be delighted to attend and said he would drop in to see his dad on the same day. We fixed it so that he would be able to take his girl, Gwen, along, as she does a lot for charity in her own way. Ken would take along a framed caricature of him and Duran which could also be raffled. The next day, early Sunday, Ken gives me a ring. "Jock a great night and well organised. We were sitting next to John Robottem the football referee." They were invited to stay overnight by the organizers, which I had previously arranged anyway. Ken continues "We are sitting down to breakfast and the hotel is beautiful and they raised a lot of money. My print went for £1,000." I had a quick word with his girl who also said it was a very good night. "Did Ken have a drink I asked"? "No," she replied so that Ken would not hear, good lad, keep it up I thought.

All stars / Broughty Ferry

I read in the courier that there was a new sports bar opening in Broughty Ferry, Dundee, so I wrote a nice wee letter to the manager, a Mr. Gordon McBean. I asked if it would it no be nice for a new club to be opened by a true sporting hero? For weeks not a thing, no letter in reply or a phone call. I had given up on this idea when out of the blue I got my reply, they would love Ken to attend and would he please bring along his belts? We agreed a fee and I made all the arrangements after speaking to Ken. During this time Ken had come to some agreement that a Mr. Rory Nichol would manage him? Mr. Nichol was not impressed with Ken working without him being aware of it. Greedy bastard. For months he said he was Kens agent without getting him any work and as soon as Ken is working, he wants a part of it? "Fuck" him I said to Ken, "This money is yours, he did fuck all to get this job," anyway all was done and dusted. I had also invited Mike along to drive and look after Kens belts. Ken picked up Mike in the town and they both came out to get me. I was still at work so, to waste time Ken produced his belts to show my work colleagues, who were over the moon.

This did the trick and I got away early, whilst Ken was signing a couple of presentations. I had a quick shower then we were off. Ken drove and he kept the roof down all the way to Broughty Ferry. It was about 30 mins driving time away, and I am sitting in the back saying "Will yi no slow down?" (Hair fucked up again.) We are going to be too early and yip, that we were, so we parked up and went to the first pub we saw. It was full of old sports photos, mostly football probably because the gentleman behind the bar was an ex Dundee United player himself.

He bought us all a drink and both Ken and Mike were on the orange and soda water whilst I had a pint. Within two minutes, other people drinking, seeing it was Ken, were over for a photo and an Autograph. It made their night and we arrived bang on time at the Sports Bar. The person who I organised the evening with was not in attendance, as he was the main manager at the Dundee branch of All Stars. A big lad on the door dressed as all bouncers, black shirt, grey blazer, sun-glasses said to go in and we would meet the organiser later. The bar was quite full, with the usual young people out on a Friday night, but it did have its fair share of older people who immediately wanted to meet Ken. There was a resident freelance photographer on hand, who was taking a lot of photos for the promotion. Ken made a nice presentation of a signed print to Jim Marr who owned the two All-stars bars and is the owner, with his brother Peter, of Dundee F.C. He was over the moon with Ken and he said that Charley, the big bouncer, would look after all, our needs.

I was not slow and letting him know we required some refreshment, no problem he says, free drink all night. (A big thanks to Mike who volunteered to be the designated driver for the night ha-ha.) We had a few drinks with Ken going outside to have his photo taken with whoever wished it and by now I am getting hungry. He says to me to ask Mike where the food is that I had told him would be on. "Fuck off, I never said anything of the kind." "Well you will have to buy us a fish supper or something." "Why me" I asked. "Well Mike has no money as he is the driver and seeing that I have not been paid yet it's down to you." "Aye ok" I said, and I tell Jimmy (Marr) we will be back in 5 minutes. "Aye no Problem son" he replied. We walked down the road looking for a chip shop and we were soon directed to a wee chippy near the promenade.

Me and Mike ordered a fish supper. "Ken, what about you" I asked? "I'll have only 10 chips as I am no too keen on them." "Yi what"? I said? "Do you honestly think the wee lassie is going to stand and count your chips?" "Yeh how no?" he replied. "Oh, look there's me on this paper" he says. Sure enough, there's Kens name promoting the opening of the bar along the road. "That's no you the lassie says." "Then who is it, honest its him" Mike says.

The owner appears and confirms it is Ken and they all wanted an Autograph. Mike produces Kens promotional cards and they are very pleased. As we walk out, I say, "How come you never said anything before I had to pay for the suppers?" "Tough" they both said as we chatted next to the water blethering about the night, which by all accounts was going well. The seagulls were having a field day with the chips that were getting launched at them and I said we better watch out that they don't shit on us. (later on, Mike noticed a big splash down his black shirt sleeve where one of the seagulls had said a thank you).

We got back to the bar and had a few more beers before telling Jim we were heading into Dundee to see the other bar. "How are yis getting there" "Oor car" I said. "No, I'll get Charlie to drive yis as it can be a bugger to park." "Aye ok," we said and jumped into the big man's car. It was braw, with a telly in the front etc. I said, "This bouncing business must pay good eh." "I don't stand on doors, I run a security door man /woman business throughout Dundee. In fact, if yis are ever in Dundee at any time I will give you my number and I will get yis into all the night clubs etc." "Braw" I replied.

We got to the Dundee All-Stars where we were met by a hand full of lads on the door, including Gordon McBean who I had initially done the paperwork with. We exchanged pleasantries and I took him to one side and gave him a signed old-fashioned boxing poster from Ken, for himself, (as Mike was coming back the next night with a lassie and I wanted him to look after him?). Wheels turning wheels eh. Ken was busy signing cards for everyone and they soon ran out, but the photographer was on hand to do the business. I met up with one of the Black Watch recruiting sergeants, Billy, who was on a night out. We also ran into, Chalky, an old pal from the Scone amateur days, a great lad and after spending at least an hour, in there we decided to get back to Broughty Ferry.

A car and driver were on hand to see us back, but not before I spoke to the manager, Gordon, about some payment. We spent another hour talking to Jimmy Marr about football etc. and then said our goodbye's, to all who looked after us. We decided to go to another bar in the Ferry with another ex BW lad on the door. He was happy for us to go into his bar and he was buying, sounds good to me I thought. Two drinks later saw us on our way back to Perth. Mike just took Kens car home to be returned the next day and Ken spent the next four days on a bender, as he said what else was there to do.

Night in the big City, Glasgow July 03

Ken phoned me and asked if he was supposed to meet me today. (That bloody memory of his). "Aye, me, Mike and a couple of the lads will be through about 2 or 3 o-clock." "Great, come and pick me up at the house and I'll take yis to the weigh in for the Fight, Scott Harrison v some Mexican lad ah Manuel Medina." Mike was round early so that he could park up his son, Brian's, car, as Brian was going to "T in the Park" and it would be safer at my hoose than in the street. I told him about the weigh in and he said it would be better if we took Georges car (4 x 4). George is a big happy go lucky man who never lets any think get him down. He left Scone years ago to take up work in the big smoke of London and during his time there, he won a good pot off money on the lottery. So, he headed back north and has been enjoying life, playing Golf, being a member of the 'Perthshire Tartan army' and travelling to all their games. He also likes having a wee drink from time to time and playing his air guitar.

So, we went round to see him. The big man was very good about it and he also produced a camera for us. So, the three of us went to my house to pick up our wee overnight bags with me driving. Then a short trip on to the Crieff road to pick up Chalky. Mike knows Chalky better than me, but what I do know about him is that he was a very good footballer. He was captain for the team me and Mike were involved with, called Scone Amateurs. He is a first one to ask when you want someone to take on a wee Jolly like this one, a very funny and genuine lad is oor Chalky. He was in good form, he is a great laugh, nothing seems to put him up or down and it took us about 45 minutes to make it to Cumbernauld. Ken was dressed and looking quite good for someone who had been on the sauce for days and I said a quick hello to Glem, Kens land lady, yi cannie get nun better.

Ken even wore this bloody silly looking black hat, tartan waste coat and scarf. He got some stick and as we entered Glasgow the nightmare started. The 'Weigh In', was being held in the Marriott hotel, but no one knew where it was. With four other drivers in the car, they were all better drivers than me (yeh right), and did they no tell me about it. After a lot of going round in circles and swearing, we eventually arrived. We were early so it was up to the bar for a pint. Ken new most of the boxers and their managers and it didn't look too organised, as Ken signed photos and did a wee interview for the TV.

I took most of the photos and got one of the Mexican challenger and a couple of group ones. We then decided to park the car up and head for the hotel that Charlie Sexton had booked for us, where we got changed and had something to eat before we started drinking again. It was only about 4 o'clock, so we were going to take it slowly as we still had to get to Sighthill for the function. But slow only lasted for two pints and then it was on to the bottles of beer, but we had a great laugh. Every pub we entered Ken was busy signing photos or getting his photo taken. We had left the good camera in the car, so George bought a disposable one and after about 6 or 8 pubs we jumped into a taxi for the function. The evening was good and Ken got up to speak and joked that he was glad he had boxed Jim (Watt) rather than his wife Margaret. Foot in mouth again but Jim took it in the spirit it was meant to be. We waited ages on a taxi back into central Glasgow where Ken and Chalky headed back to the hotel, whilst me, George and Mike went to the dancing. I had one more beer and held my hand up and said I have had my fill and walked back to the hotel, leaving the two young lads to it at around Two o'clock in the morning.

We were awakened by a knock on our door by a woman saying it was time to check out. Nine o'clock, are you mad woman? "That's early is it no" says George. "We best get sorted and head out" I replied. We couldn't get the shower to work so we went along to Mikes and Chalkys room to find them running about naked and sorting them self's out. Ken sat and watched the golf on the TV patiently waiting for us. What must he think about this crazy lot eh? Soon after we got the owner to take a photo of us outside the hotel, said our goodbyes and headed into the centre for breakfast, where we eventually got something at the train station. Chalky was dying for a pint and Mike said he would drive, good lad. There after we really got stuck into the beer, walking all around the big city, we were determined to enjoy our self, as we rarely get in to Glasgow.

We dropped Ken of somewhere as he was heading out to see a woman, then dropped Chalky of at a lassies house and took the car back to Georges flat, where we had more drink. I got home late, and the wife went daft. But after 28 years marriage I had heard it all before. So, I took my ear bashing and went to bed, another great day, (oh and Scott Harrison got beat on points).

Burns pub Perth. Opening 25th July 03

At the start of May I was asked by an old friend, Greg Keenan, who is manager of Tay Bank Tavernier's in Perth and owns a number of pubs in the Perth and Kinross area, if Ken would like to open his pub. The pub, "The Robert Burns" was opening in July and he would make it a wee fundraiser for me. I said, "Aye I will have a word with the man." (Greg has always been good with me regarding charity events). Ken said "Aye" and that was it, I was just to sort out timings etc.

So, as the time got nearer Ken phoned me up and said "Jock I dinnae think I will be able to make your opening night at the Burns as Rory said it would conflict with contracts he had made with other businesses in the toon." "Fuck him, get him to phone me asap." Sure enough he phoned me, we exchanged words and I told him my plans, in the end Ken did make it on the night. "I'll be in suit and tie, is that ok" Ken said? "Aye sure both Mike and me will be in casual kit." "Be smart then he said" Cheeky bugger. As normal he phoned me on the night just to make sure he was going the right way. "Aye right oh", he turns up almost on time after being at a meeting with Rory. He is dressed in a casual shirt and he brought along a nice print for Greg but left it for me as mine was already made out for Greg and his wife Margaret. He also left me the first photo of a limited-edition print, number 1 of 30, signed with the words "To my big buddy Jock", which was very good of him.

So, we jumped in his car as he was not drinking and went round and collected Sandy McDuff, who was in the process of getting dressed when we arrived. Just in time as it happens as he was putting on this Salmon colour shirt. "Yir no going oot with that on, have yi no got a better one" I says? Sandy changed whilst we waited, then it was up for big George Smith. As we waited for him, we had a bottle of beer and George phoned Mike to say we would meet him in Christy's. We walked in to see Mike already there shouting the drinks in, good lad I thought. After a quick one in there, it was then round to the Royal for a quick half pint where Ken insisted, he would buy them. Fuck of Ken yir only on soft drinks, we will get them in, and after 5 minutes Arguing it was settled and I got the round.

And no, it wasn't my round as it was only half's we had robbed Ken again. We then all marched into the Burns, it's only a wee place but tonight it seemed tiny as it was packed to the roof. I made my way with Ken and the lads to the back of the pub and signalled to Greg to join us whereupon I introduced Ken to Him and Margaret. Ken did the presentation to them, of the print, and Greg took me outside and gave me money for Ken and said there will be a raffle for me later in the night. Nice one.

I passed Ken his money whereupon he tried to stick notes into my pocket. "What the hell are you doing, its your cut Ken." "Bugger off he said." "I got money from Greg didn't I Sandy" I replied gesticulating to Sandy, who was looking on. "Oh, aye he did that" Sandy said, lying through his teeth lol. Greg took a lot of photos with Ken and his belts outside the pub with the locals who wanted it, this was after Ken went behind the bar and did his work with the 4 belts in his hands. We stayed for about an hour when Kens phone went. It was Rory. "I have been here an hour" Ken said. Turning to me he said, "Rory said I was not to stay too late." "Tell him to go and take a running fuck to himself the wee shit" I replied. "No, its ok Jock" said the man.

I didn't want to say too much, so after ten more minutes, we said oor goodbyes to Greg and the locals. We headed off round to another one of Greg's pubs, The Thistle, to get him to draw a couple of raffles. Mike won one but we put the prize back into the raffle, poor sod. We again said our goodbyes and I walked Ken back to his car, where he drove back to the Burns, said more goodbyes and thanked them for the night, before heading off down the Glasgow road. In the meantime, I headed back for some more refreshments with the lads. Me and the lads stayed for a wee while, Mike and George did there bit by winning at the raffle, and I had made a few bob for my charity, which I was to pick up on the Sunday after my training walk. That was about it for me, and Sandy headed back to his hoose where he quickly fell asleep, so I went home, as Mike and George went to Superstars dancing.

Photos

Me, Ken, Colin Jones, (British, Commonwealth and
European welterweight champion) and Phil Jones

Me leading off against RAF champion,
Ballykinlar N Ireland

My Bro willie, brother-in-law Jimmy T, me,
Ken, Marshall Colman

Ken, Phil Jones, me and Dick McTaggart
British ex boxer's hall of fame

Mike Scott, Robert Thomson (RIP) Me,
Jimmy T, Ken. My 50th

Sahara Charity Walk finished. Where's the pub?

Me, Ken, Dod Mcluskie, Bayview,Methil

Tom McPherson, Me, Ken,
Stuart (My hoose)

Take that: Central Bar, Leith Walk, Edinburgh

Grandson Callum, & granddaughter Eilidh,
with the MBE medals

Mike Scott, Ken, Me Glasgow

My Dad

Round 5

"To be a boxer is to be within yourself, inside your
thoughts and feelings." - Brian D'Ambrosio

Kens Dinner Dundee / 50 years in Boxing

Ken phoned me up one day and said that Rory was thinking about
organizing a dinner, for him, to celebrate his 50 years in boxing, good
idea I thought. "I will get him to send you out some paperwork on the
idea" Ken said. Great I thought I just hope it goes better than the one in
Glasgow. A few days later a letter arrived on my doorstep from Rory. I
looked through it. It was amateur from the start to finish, bad grammar
and poor spelling, all in all it was pish, (me the English teacher? lol). I
phoned Ken and said that I have read his handy work and went through it
with him. I also said that I had sent out a letter to Rory explaining what a
poor effort it was and he should let Ken or someone with a little more
nous than him, proof read it before it goes out again. Later Ken had a
meeting with Rory in Perth, and Rory said that he thinks we are getting
at him.

Fuck me Ken if he puts out that shit he deserves it, don't you think?
The long and the short of it is a dinner is being organised for Ken on the
26th of September at the Hilton in Dundee, that will put a few noses out
in the capital (Edinburgh) after this? I was tasked to sell 10 tickets which
was no problem. I handpicked the lads I wanted to sit with all night and

no doubt through to the wee hours of Saturday morning. I organised a wee minibus, through a good local guy by the name of "Jock the Jannie" who also, in his spare time, drives the Dundee F.C. supporters (Perth Branch), to all their games. He has driven with my pals before on a wee trip to Methil, but that's another story to be spoke about at the bar. We came to an agreement about the cost which would be £10 per head to Dundee and back, which I thought was a good number. Jock will get a wee free beer for his trouble and whilst I'm speaking about free beers, everyone who climbs aboard the bus with me will get the same.

I brought a colour copy of a framed print pencil drawing, which me and Ally Alcorn had commissioned, for Ken from the Buchanan clan, to celebrate his 50 years in the game. Plus, a couple of extra ones for oor welsh brother Phil, Kens son and Dad. Am I no a generous wee lad? I meet George at his flat at 1:30pm, to hand over a pair of cufflinks which he needed and then it's a taxi into the town to finish of photo copying of extra prints. We then meet most of the lads in Christies pub at 2pm for a couple of hours, inducting our bellies to the foaming ale, before boarding the minibus outside Christies at 4pm, to head into Dundee. More refreshments, then meet up with Mickey Douglas who is arriving by train, then to the venue to meet Ken for about 7pm.

We all had a great time. Yip, we all thoroughly enjoyed our self's from start to finish. A couple of the big named guests did not turn up, John H Stacy and Alan Minter to name but a few, but Big Ernie Shavers made up for them and he was first class. All the guests could not do enough to please everyone in attendance and at one stage I was even given the microphone to say a couple of words. Me and Mike chipped in 320 quid each to buy Mikes sister in law a signed boxing glove, which we presented to her husband Dave and he was over the moon. I don't recall ever getting on the minibus for the return journey, but hey whats knew? The sad thing about it all is Ken again is not going to see a penny from all this.

One of the guests was mad Frankie Fraser. An English gangster and criminal who spent a total of 42 years in prison for numerous violent offences. Fraser was part of Britain's underworld between the 1940s-1960's. He was a known associate of gangster Billy Hill throughout the 1950s. Frankie had 10 years added to a sentence he was serving in 1967, along with The Richardson Brothers, in the Torture Trials which were the longest trials in British criminal history. Fraser knew the Kray twins well and attended all the Kray brother's funerals. He also sat with Reggie Kray on his deathbed in 2000 and he himself died in 2014 of complications from surgery. He was sitting talking to someone, when me and Mike asked if he didn't mind signing a few programmes for the lads. "No problem he says" speaking in a broad London accent. I said "Can I ask you a question?" "Yes, please go ahead." I said "what are you so mad about? (He is called mad Franky after all). He laughed and said, "It's an old nick name son," and just looked at me with one of those looks that said no more questions ok? We said thanks and got back to our night.

Rory said that he sold quite a few tickets to various companies and people, who never actually turned up on the evening. So, he had to pay for the lost meals himself. This is the man who sent out paperwork saying that all tickets were to be paid up front and he never even checked out the people or companies beforehand. Yes, he put on a good night, but he stated in his paperwork that all money raised during the raffle and the auction would all go towards Ken. Shit, full of wind and pish. Yet again the man (Ken) gets a kick in-between the legs. Ken deliberately went on the piss for a few days after this and who could blame him. Every time Rory tried to speak to him, he got an ear bashing. Rory then started phoning me, at all hours, asking what he should do and at the same time trying to explain the loss to me. I told him to leave Ken alone for a couple of weeks and if he ever wanted to speak to him again, he would do it in his own time no one else's, so fuck off.

It didn't help matters with Ken getting a shite letter from his son Mark to deal with but that's another story. It's a father and son thing which I will not go in to, so we will leave this to one side eh? Rory sent a printout to Ken, with a full break down of outgoings and incomings from the function, with only one or two receipt's, but this did not pacify Ken who will nail the wee shit one way or another. Rory is a great talker and likes to be around people, i.e. the centre of attention and I feel he has let Ken down. Rory has been on the phone to me over the last few nights, sometimes phoning quite late, asking if I have been in contact with Ken, and what has he been saying, as if I would tell him. I basically said Ken is taken some time out and will phone him when he feels like it, not when anyone else says, so don't bother him for at least a couple of weeks, this information of course was relayed straight to Ken.

Ken, true to his word did take time out, and had a good couple of weeks in the pub. I spoke with him on the odd occasion, mostly when he phoned me late in the night, but hey what are pals for? If yi can't speak to someone you just bottle it up. I did manage to get Ken to put a few dates in his diary, which were mostly social nights up in my area. So, if he wants to get drunk great, but I would prefer it was where I can see him, due to there being a lot of spongers in his own pub. Yes, there are some very good genuine lads, like big Tam who know Ken well and does look after him, but there are the ones who would take advantage of Kens good nature. As I batter out this line, Ken is down in Wales with his welsh brother Phil Jones, at a civic reception for him and Emile Griffith, to name but a few. He is well looked after down there. Oor Welsh brothers know true legends when they see one. We in Scotland only pay lip service to this, we don't really appreciate it.

Ken had a lot of paperwork that Rory had sent him, regarding print out of expenditure etc. from the function. Ken phoned me at work to ask if I had a spare Dundee programme, where I reminded him that I did not get one and that he said he would get me one? I said I would ask Mike to give him a bell tomorrow, as he probably had one. We also spoke briefly, about a night of amateur boxing in Kinross, which the organiser had mentioned to Ken during the Dundee evening. Ken said he would go, but didn't know the full details and he asked if I could phone them up and get the low down for him?

I phone up the organiser who said it was to be a Scotland v England match, with Dick McTaggart, Tommy Gilmour, and Ken being at the top table with dinner suit or Kilt Order being the dress? I asked about a fee. He said both the other guests are doing it for nothing. I said Ken would not, this being his only income. He said, "What about £100?" I said "Yeh, what about it?" I told him that If you want Ken at the top table you are going to have to do better than that, you are going to make a small fortune with the items you will be raffling and auctioning, plus you have already said in the local paper that Ken will be appearing. I will speak with Ken, but I want to come to some arrangement with you regarding a percentage of the items Ken will bring to the night to be raffled or auctioned, to make up for the lack of money up front. So, I told him I would see what Ken has to say today about it, today being the 25thOctober 2003. The boxing night was scheduled for the 7th November 2003.

Well I had a call from the man (Ken) last night, 3rd November about 10pm. He said I was to swear not to mention what he was about to tell me which sounds ominous. He said he had been speaking to Rory and that Duran was coming to the UK some time in February next year and he will be taking part in an exhibition boxing match. Ken said he will be boxing him, which will not be sanctioned by the B.B.B. of C. (British Boxing Board of Control). I said, "I should hope not you are 58 not fucking 28, and yis should both know better, yi could do yourself some damage." Ken said "I'll be ok, I will get into training. Would you come down to London with me?" "Aye sure" I said hoping that this will all disappear in smoke and talk as time passes. "You, Rory, and Glem are the only people who know about this, so please don't say a thing, if the papers hear about this, fuck knows what will be said. I'm looking to be making a good few bob oot of this." "Aye and what about Rory" I said? "Don't you worry about him I will watch his every move; you can be assured of that?"

I will speak to Ken when I see him on Friday, 7th November at the Scotland v England select boxing show, about this and the health side of this adventure. What will people make of this? Ken has in fact got a broken back and that is why he can't work. Has Rory taken this into consideration? So, we will see what he says. I would prefer that he did his own thing and tell Rory to get to fuck and have nothing to do with him, still nothing is plane sailing when yir Ken Buchanan, aye yir some man.

Maxwell's Boxing show

My wee nephew, Sean, phoned me up one evening and said that his boxing coach, wants Kens number to ask if he would attend a boxing show in Methil, on 18th February 2004. "No Sean" I said "I can't give out Kens number like that" (if he phoned Ken his self, knowing Ken he would attend and would only take petrol money, his hearts to bloody big).

So, I got his boxing coach to phone me to make the arrangements. We had a blether, and the bottom line is Ken was going to the show. He phoned me the night before saying what time he would arrive at my house and that his son Mark would also be coming, which was fine by me. As I put down the phone my wee nephew, Sean, phoned? "Uncle John I am no going back to the boxing?" he said. "Ok what's happened" I asked. "Well Tommy, the boxing coach, never said thank you to me for giving him your number, so that Ken could attend the boxing show, and I have to still pay to get in" he replied. Question, "Sean, did you like the boxing?" "Aye all my pals go", "fine go back to the boxing." Listen, this is what's going to happen tomorrow when we come through. You be ready and you will drive to the show in a big flash BMW (he likes his cars), and you will go in with us, so that you don't have to pay. All your pals and your coach will see that you have arrived in style and know Ken better that any one in attendance. "Ok" he said. "Any way Sean, you will find in life not every buddy is like you, brought up to say please and thank you, life's not like that."

Ken and Mark arrived on time, and not one call from Ken to say where do I go. Makes a change eh? They were in Marks big top of the range BMW sports car, so Sean will be over the moon. Right, first stop, into the town to see a man about a camera. I'd had a phone call from the manager

Robb Hall, off 'Snappy Snaps', which is a photo developing shop in the town. He said he would donate 3 underwater cameras for me to take to the Sahara Desert (charity walk). Yeh, I know what you are thinking, underwater, the desert, it doesn't make sense, but if you think about it, it does? Anyway, during our conversation, he said he was a big boxing fan, so here's Ken arriving on his doorstep to meet him. He also had along his belts, surprise, surprise. I made the introductions and we went outside for two minutes of posing. Robb was brilliant and he gave Ken a large photo frame for one of his prints and a large disposable camera for the raffle at the show we were attending, a really nice Englishman.

Soon we were on our way to Methil. Just before we got about five miles from my sisters, I phoned to say where we were and can we have some toast and coffee when we arrive. "Aye nae bother" she said, good lass. So, we sat, had oor coffee whilst Sean got ready, had a wee chat with my mum who always comes up to Janet's for Sunday dinner, and then we were off. Sean got in the front with Mark driving of course, and me and Ken in the back, yi couldn't slap the smile of Sean's face if you had hit him in the face with a Kipper. We arrived with time to spare. Maxwell's is a big nightclub, in the area with a good few boozers on hand, Sunday or not. We met Tommy the coach, who was running the show and he ushered us to a waiting table. "Right Sean you head of with yir pals and I will see you from time to time, yeh right?" I went to the bar and got three pints of water with some orange squash. Yip it was to be a dry day, (will make up for it later) and Ken was busy signing autographs for everyone and there dug.

Wee Sean brought his pal up to get his photo taken with Ken. Not once did Ken say "Bugger off and geese piece. "He was the centre of attention and so he should be, the perfect guest to everyone, even the drunks. The boxing soon got started, young laddies first, 6 bouts, then the interval. Ken was asked to pick out the first raffle ticket. I had bought us five all together, but I don't know why I buy any for Ken, he always puts what he wins back in again, (bloody sure I widdnae). He got up into the ring to explain how and when he won his 4 belts, as Mark handed them up to his dad. The punters loved it and after about 10 minutes he left the ring to a standing ovation.

The auction was next with Kens gloves going for about £130, with all the money going to the boxing club funds, so they must have raised easily £600 in total. The rest of the bill, 6 more bouts, were all wars, not a lot of skill, i.e. blocks (unless you count the nose?), parry's, slips etc. but the punters watching on were shouting their heeds aff. It was great entertainment, aye the Methil area folk enjoy a good punch up, but it's no pretty to watch. During this battle, my big bro, Willie, walked in, seen what was going on and said, "Hi Jock when's the boxing starting." Aye yir no wrang. He said hi to Ken and I introduced him to Mark and he then went off to the bar. I went up with him for a wee natter, then headed off to speak to some old regimental pals.

I even met some old school mates, Christ do I no look good in comparison (or am I just kidding myself)? So, with the boxing / war over I steered Ken over to say goodbye to the organizers, said bye to Sean and my bro and headed back to Perth and soon arrived at the lodge in Scone. Nope not a real shock eh, as we had a quick pint with the lads who all know Ken well. Ken gave me a cuddle, Mark shook my hand, said thanks for the day and headed oot the door. Me well I stayed oot and got hammered, (well drunk).

By, By Laurence of Fife?

The week before my epic adventure into the Sahara Desert Ken decides to phone me. "Jock, when are you away on your wee trip." "I fly next Friday Ken." "So this weekend will be the last time you'll get oot for a pint?" "Yip, yir right." "Ok, I will see you on Saturday and we can go oot for a few." "Aye that will be braw." On the Friday, about 11:30am the phone goes, its Ken. "What time did I say I would be round again?" "5pm at my house" I said. His voice seems lost somehow, (he was looking for some company). "If you want you can come around earlier if you have nothing on" I said. "Aye that would be great, what time?" "12:30pm at Duffy's, me, you and Mike can head up the A9 to Aberfeldy to watch my amateur team play, if yir up for it." "Aye ok." I phoned Mike to let him know what was happening and arranged for Mike to be at Duffy's early just in case Ken turned up early. As I was picking up three cameras from a sponsor, Mike phoned to say that Ken was on time and he had just got a pint in for him at Duffy's, but Ken could not find a parking space. "It's ok" I said, tell him to meet me at my house.

I arrived just as Ken was getting out of his car and two minutes later we are picking up Mike and heading down the A9 to watch Letham Amateurs play football at Dunkeld. We got there in plenty of time. Mike and Ken stayed in the car whilst I went and spoke with the team, (they would not get oot the car, it was to bloody cold). Once the game got under way, they both stood at the side lines and watched as we started to get to grips with the opposition. By half time we are 2-0 up, so I went round to speak with Mike and Ken, but I should not have bothered. All I got was "Yir team is shite, you said they were good." Mike, yip he knows football but Ken a hearts supporter, "Fuck off" was my reply. Anyway, we thumped them, but I can't remember the score. We head back with me still getting pelters and go to my house, so we could leave the car and walk, surprise, surprise, to the lodge to have a quick pint before the bus arrives. As normal the crack is good with me still getting pelters.

Mike phones for "Jock the boxs" taxi firm. Thank fuck it's on time I am thinking, I can't take all this pish. We head straight for the 'Whitty' (White Horse pub) that sponsor my amateur team and we carry on where we left off in the lodge but staying on the bottled beer. We have a good few then we start taking photos with Ken and the players. who are well chuffed. For the next stop, its off to Mikes club 'The civil service club', where we sit and watch off all things, Boxing. Three bottles later we head back into the town just as I got a phone call from Bob, one of the team, to ask what oor plans were. Drinking of course, obviously lol. We meet up at the 'Thistle pub' and drink buckets load of beer. The lads were in great form, well up for a pint and we had a great night. But all good thinks come to an end, i.e. Ken said, "Right bedtime wee man I am fucked." So, we got our self's in to yet another taxi and went home, yet another bloody good night was had.

Legends night. 15/05/04

It was during a routine pint in the watering hole that is 'The Lodge', that the new man in the chair, Jimmy Napier, asked me if Ken did any after dinner speaking. "Oh, Christ aye he does, how" I asked? "If we were to sit down and have a pint later on in the week to discuss a Sportsman's night, would you ask Ken if he would be the main speaker?" "Aye that's fine with me. "So with diary in hand, I head of to the lodge the following week. Sandy was going down under (New Zealand) so me, Jimmy, and Frazier sat down and worked out the primaries, i.e. date, dress, price of tickets, attendance numbers etc. I checked with Ken if the date was ok and he said aye. I said a fee, again he was happy. 75 tickets to be sold should be easy? Right the next step was to get someone along to speak with Ken.

I had asked Ken if Dick McTaggart spoke at dinners, but he said, "No, he's no in good health at the moment and he lives a good bit away." So I thought to myself, what about a saint Johnston player and I put out the feelers but nah, to dear, greedy bastards. I put this dilemma to a good contact I have on the papers by the name of Jim Mason, a fantastic man with a head full of boxing knowledge. "I have a pal who does stand-up comedy, he is great, Bruce Fummey is his name. I will put it to him if you want" he said. "Great" I replied. The long and the short of the story is, I now have Ken speaking, along with Bruce doing a stint and with Jim himself doing the master of ceremonies, so game on. I arranged a wee meeting with, Jim Napier, Frazer Mitchell from across the road, who was the lodges money man, and myself to sort out who was getting paid what and timings. Basically, the programme and who was to sort out tickets.

I went along to see Bill Anderson who ran Perth Railway boxing club, and asked if he would speak to his boxers about the function and could I put up a poster up with details on it? I did the same with Letham FC, the club I coach, and phoned a few others. So, things were going ok and a week before the function I organised another meeting, same folk plus Sandy, to find out ticket sales are no going to well Jock. We had only sold about 20 tickets. Fuck me, I thought, that's no good I am going to have to push this. So, I spoke about how it must go ahead due to me not wanting to look a cunt and having to phone Ken, Bruce and Jim up, to say it's off at this late stage. So, it was a case of let's get on the phone to every cunt and sell tickets, (mind you, there was a couple in the lodge who did not want this to be a success?) Are they no meant to support the man in the chair? So we decided that the show must go on. I went up to Pitlochry with Mike one Saturday to watch my amateurs and see if they wanted any more tickets, rather than go on a march with the Black Watch association on the same day. Some folk weren't happy but selling tickets was a bigger priority than marching round Perth with the British legion, on this occasion. On the Thursday before the function, I had said I would go to the lodge and help set up the function hall upstairs.

As I was heading to the Lodge, I bumped into Sandy who was on his way down to open up, he was half few? (Drunk). "Where the hell have you been" I asked? "Up at Ken Smiths, his sister has just died so Frazer and me went round to see him and drank a bottle? Is that ok?" "Fine by me pal" I said. We opened the lodge and had a pint before starting on the job in hand then Frazer arrived. So, Sandy sits on his arse and runs the bar, whilst me and Frazer get on with the work. I was instructed to do something just now and come upstairs in a wee while by Frazer. (Must be letting the goat oot for a piss I thought?). So, I got on with the business downstairs of putting up posters, which I had blown up, of Ken and his titles, and the programmes to begin with, then after a while I went up to help oot Frazer.

"What a hell of a lot of stuff Frazer" I said as we started moving some stuff away, "aye and bloody heavy" I continued. After about an hour's work I said my goodbyes and told him, that I would be back in in the morning with more posters etc. It's a great excuse for a pint, you know me. There was not much to do on the Friday with Jim Napier, Allan Machatie and Ken Smith all helping out, not forgetting Sandy putting his two pence worth in. So, "All is looking braw and all we need is a good turn oot" I said. "Aye we will get that" they all replied, I wish I had their faith. Saturday seen me head oot to '7 acres' to warm up my amateurs, who were playing in a semi-final and Stuart, my young lad (daddy to be), and Mike turned up whilst I was in the midst of giving them a lengthy warm up. Stuart was only after a key to pick up mail.

We don't see as much of him now that he has another family in Airdrie. Still, the mother of his sons and hopefully daughters need him more at the moment and he has been with me and his mum for over 27 years, so we need a break, lol naw. Mike said the warmup was too long, pish, they bloody need it. They start of too slow and take until the last 20 minutes to get into the game. I was right, they hammered their opponents, Burrilton, 8-1, a great result, now let's get changed and get pissed I thought. When I got home there was two messages for me. The first was from Robb the manager of 'Snappy Snaps,' the camera shop in the town. Him and his work colleague would love to turn up as my guest but will have to turn up straight from work. So, I quickly call him. "Yip, great, see yis both at 7:00pm for7:30pm" I said. The other was from Ken, asking me to call him. "Fuck I hope this is not a call off."

It wasn't, he was just saying, him and Mark were leaving Edinburgh at 5pm and should be with me for 6pm, aye, I will no hud my breath. Sitting changed and nursing a coffee waiting for them to turn up, I hear what I think is a tank roar in to oor wee road. What the fuck is that I am thinking? Looking out I see Mark parking up his big blue BMW top of the range sport car. They both look smart and we all shake hands and settle down with a coffee to wait for Bruce the comedian to arrive. "Nay biscuits" Ken says, "piss poor hoose this is it no?" Not once, but a couple of times. Fuck it, I sneak oot and drive up to the spar and get a couple of packets for them. "Here's yir biscuits yi moaning bugger." Ken by now has signed all the prints (raffle prizes) and I get a call from Bruce, he's lost, so I go out into the street to talk him in.

He arrives dressed in kilt and a loud, bright T-shirt and he's no skinny, in fact he is bloody massive. I introduce him to Mark and Ken. I jump in Bruce's car with the other two following us down to the lodge and we arrive to see that the place is only half full. Christ, I hope this gets better I thought to myself. I get Jim Napier over to meet Mark, Ken and Bruce and ask him to look after them whilst I sort oot the raffle and speak to some of the lads. Sandy comes up stairs to get me. "Jock did you book a Photographer" he asks?" "Aye I did" I reply." "Well he is down stairs looking for you." "Great, so I get all the top table guests upstairs for a photo session, and to think I thought the 'Perthshire Advertiser' rep would not turn up, well done.

After about 30 minutes, downstairs is packed, what a great turn oot. Both Sandy and Jim are happy, thank fuck. I have a quick word with Jim Mason about the programme and he is happy, a very flexible lad. I tell Sandy and Jim that we will give them about 30 minutes at the bar, then we will ask them to make their way upstairs, whilst in the meantime Jim gets his own photographer to take a photo for the 'Evening telegraph.' It's good to see some of the team from Letham arrive in good spirits, with an 8-1 victory they should be too. So, about 30 minutes later Jim has his gavel in his hand and is getting everyone's attention and after everyone has taken their seat upstairs, Sandy leads the top table upstairs, to loud applause. I sit at the back of the hall with Mark, and Jim introduces the top table to the audience, this is kick off. Bruce is first up and is he no great, everyone was laughing their heads aff. He can grip an audience and for about thirty minutes he does his stuff. Then Jim gets them to retire downstairs for a gentleman's break and get something to eat, and of course, refill oor glasses, whilst I get time to speak to a couple of my own guests.

Gregg Keenan, Ken McKenzie, the lads from Snappy Snaps and the football lads were putting the drink away in good style, its amasing what a good win does for moral. I managed to have a quick word with Ken about his plans. "I am moving in with Mark. He has a beautiful penthouse in Leith and he will be running my affairs from now on" he says. "Great" I said but I was not too sure about this move. Mark is a good lad, but at his age should he no be oot looking for a life of his own, and no be living with his dad? I really hope it works out, but what about his lass in the west and what about his land lady, Glem, who has been looking after him for about seven years? She is a great woman, but this is no the time to get into this, it was time for everyone to get back upstairs. When all was seated Jim introduced Ken to a fantastic response.

Ken started off by producing one of the old posters I had put up around the lodge. "Jock can you come up here a minute" says Ken. What is this all about I thought, so he spoke briefly about when he boxed my dad and a wee bit about my own boxing days, then pulled out one of his own amateur boxing cards (1964-1965, 20 contests & 20 wins). It was the one with my dad's name on it and, Bayview, the home of my own club, East Fife. He then presented the card to me saying "Keep this as a wee memento." (Was this no a goodbye present?). I wasn't going to take it at first, as it is a peace of Kens fantastic career, but I accepted it and turned to walk back to my seat with a big cheer in my ear, it will look great framed in Stuarts new house I thought to myself, thanks Ken. Ken spoke for about 20 minutes, then he made a wee story out of each belt as he produced them. He always starts out quiet then gets a wee bit louder and louder. A short informal interview was supposed to be next with Jim asking Ken questions, but the punters took over by asking questions to Ken about events throughout his boxing career. Soon there were more and more lads wanting to ask their own questions and Ken was very positive and honest with everyone. He even took time out to slag me off about showing my knob to Duran lol, and the punters were really enjoying the crack, as is the way with Ken Buchanan.

I went to the back of the room and gave Jim a signal to bring the questions to an end, so that they could get their photos taken with Ken and the belts. Mark was up helping his dad, so I took time out to get to the bar before the rush started. The drink was flowing, and the crack was great. Everyone was in good spirits and Ken looked at me as if to say I wish I could stay on. After about 30 minutes Ken cuddled me and said keep in touch wee man whilst Mark shook my hand and said thanks. I handed Ken an envelope with his fee in it, and he never has to count it. As he walked out, I thought I hope I do see him again.

Bruce the great comedian said his goodbyes and I passed him his fee, again no need to check it. He made a lot of contacts, and he handed out his card on a number of occasions, so well worth what he got paid, bloody good if you ask me. My evenings work is done I thought as I stole time out to speak with my old pal Mike. All of a sudden, I was directed over into a corner by lads from the football team and sat down with a good spread of nips in front of me. Fergie, the manager, said he has signed the lads he wanted signed but still wanted me to say I will be with them next year? Not before saying I was one of the top amateur football coaches in Perthshire. Fuck me where is Mike when I want him, he should be hearing this. Well what could I say, but off course I will, with one or two demands by the way lol. Enough said, let's get back to the bar, and we did with vengeance.

Jim Mason thanked me for my work and said he had a taxi waiting, "Don't forget your presentation I said." "What presentation Jock?" Oh Fuck, Ken has forgot to present it to him. Quick upstairs I said, we both rush upstairs, and I produced a framed photo of Ken with a nice wee piece at the bottom saying congratulations on your appointment as the new master of Scone lodge, he was over the moon. I said it was my mistake I should have remembered. The football lads and Mike took off in a taxi to head back into the town and the White Horse, for more drink. The bar was closing, why I thought, Christ its after 2:30am, I better get my arse up the road. Still time for a quick drink with Sandy, eh no sorry I can't, he is sleeping again, what a lad.

Any way it was a great night, I hope I get a look at the many photos that were taken. The following day, when I got home from work, there was a message on my answering machine from Glem, Kens land lady," Jock give me a wee call please darling?"

Round 6 🥊

"We all fight for money, some for power, but most of all for love. But me, I fight to become a champion." - Jonathan Anthony

Small Talk

"Hi Glem, its Jock." "Oh hi, how did your night go." Small talk, small talk. "Jock, did Ken stay over with you?" "No, he went back to Edinburgh with Mark." "Jock I think he is going to stay with Mark from now on?" "Well he never said that to me in so many words, (trying to stay on both sides here). Glem you will have to tie him down and speak to him when you can," I said. "It's no fair, I have a lot to speak to him about, rent, that wee bastard Rory etc," Glem said. "Glem, if he was to move out he will sit down and speak with you first" I said, (fuck I hope so) this could go on and on. Well, I got a phone call from Glem the following week, "Jock the wee mans moved oot" she said, "he emptied his room last week." "What did he say?" "Well we sat Doon for about three hours and spoke through a lot of things. He was with me for over seven years Jock and I told him how much he owed me in back rent. He wanted me to keep my voice down as his shadow, Mark, was in the next room and he said he will come back next week to paint oot his room for me. I'll miss him Jock."

"I don't want to let his room just in case he does want to come back, but I cannie leave it empty for too long, as I need the rent money even more now. Don't you worry I'll keep in touch with you and Christine. Oh, what did Mark have to come up here for and spoil things and what will Kens dad (Tommy) say? He will no be happy aboot Ken leaving here" she said.

Well what could I say? Ken said he would never ever stay in Edinburgh, after the way they treated him. I told her not to worry, if it was meant to be it was meant to be, (What shite is that?) Maybe we are both being selfish, and it is a good turn for Ken, as Mark says he will keep him (his dad) off the drink, yeh right. As long as Ken is happy about what he is doing it is fine by me, but I am aware I will not be seeing much of Ken now that he is in the capital, is this the end of the book already? Fuck knows but I hope not, he is still my good pal whatever direction he takes.

Well, Ken did get back to paint oot the room as promised. Out of the blue Ken phones me one night and he starts of by putting on an English accent. "Hi Ken, how are you" I say? "How did yi ken it was me? I'm in a restaurant with Gully having a birthday meal hint-hint, it's great, how have you been. I have been trying to get in touch with you, is your number 552656?" Wrong, I mean to say how many times has he been phoning my house? "Ken, have you no got a landline installed?" "No, I haven't even got my mail redirected here, I'm not sure what I am doing but it will be sorted by September though?" What this only means god knows. I reminded Ken about missing Mike Scott's grandsons christening, and not being at the regimental day.

"I forget about that" says Ken. But he does sound happy, so, we chatted for about 20 minutes, thank fuck it's no my phone. We ended saying keep in touch and true to his word he phones me out of the blue as I am watching the football. Does he no watch the euro 2004 games I thought, as we made small talk. "Where are you then" I say. "Am in a

Chinese restaurant having a great meal and a nice wee glass of red wine." "Is Mark no with you then?" "No, he is down south, (cats away springs to mind and he sounds very happy). I am off to London soon for the British Boxing Board of Controls anniversary, not sure what one?" "Are they paying the flight etc." "Are they fuck. I have to pay the lot, accommodation as well. Yir wee pal Charlie Magri (held WBC and lineal flyweight titles) will be there, I will tell him you said hallo eh"

"Will you be my guest at a wee do next month" I ask, "I'll send you the information through the post." "Hey where's my birthday card you wee bugger?" "Ken where would I send it? You haven't given me your address yet?" "I'll send my new address on a post card to you if I can remember your address, in fact let's see if you get it if I only write, to Jock Mcinnes, ugliest man in Scone on it?" Oh, Aye I I'll get it awe right.

"Have you met any old Edinburgh pals since returning to the capital Ken, I ask?" "Aye sure I have" Ken replies. "Do they still remember you?" "Jock I canny get peace wherever I go." "Ken the time to be pissed off is when they forget you, when they ask you for your autograph or photo it's just there way of saying thanks for the memories eh" Again we spoke for a while. "Jock, did you phone me, or did I phone you?" "You phoned me Ken." "Oh right I must be going" he says with a big laugh, but still he keeps on chatting about his meal. "You should taste this chicken Jock, or you would like this beautiful red wine." Fuck me he does go on. "So, your no watching the game then Ken." "Nope" came the reply, so I said I will go and watch the second half and have a beer and think about him. "Aye you do that and say hallo to your wife from me and Stuart, love you Jock byeeeeeeee."

Small Talk

A short time after, maybe the 26 or 27 of July, Glem phoned me. She was very upset as her brother had died and she had to tell me. She said Ken was also told and he got upset as well as he knew the old lad. I phoned her a couple of times after this to find out how she was bearing up. She sounded ok, big strong women this is. It was about a week after this I got home from a shit day at work for Christine to say that Glem had called. I stopped what I was doing and returned her call. "He's home" she said.

Ken had phoned her, and they spoke about him getting his old room back. "Great" I said, not wanting to go into detail, I said I would give him a call later and so I did. "Hey big boy what are you up to?" "Oh no much what about you." I explained I had a Fife team visiting Perth to play oor Letham team. "Oh, that sounds all right." "Hey what about me picking you about 10am Saturday morning, drive through to Perth, do a wee bit of shopping then head on to the game down near oor North Inch, then have a meal and a couple of pints?" "Aye sure that sounds great." Unbeknown to him I had phoned a couple of reporters and said that Ken was disgusted by the governments plans to disband my old regiment the Black Watch and that he was on his way to the Headquarters of the regiment to sign a petition to that fact. Sure enough, they were up for a reporter and a photographer to be there for Kens visit.

I told Ken of my wee plan after I had picked him. At the castle (HQ), the two photographers were there and a good pal of oors, Jim Mason, from the 'Evening Telegraph.' The local Fife /Dundee paper, 'The Courier', wanted Ken holding a recent edition of the paper, whilst wearing a Blue bonnet. Me and Ken were annoying each other and having a wee laugh. "Jock will yi get me a blue bonnet?" "Aye sure Ken." Into the castle shop I go and come back with the smallest bonnet I could get my hands on. It was like a wee boy's school cap, very small on his head. "I cannie wear this" he shouts. "Sorry Ken it's all they have" (I lie through · my teeth). He gets his photo taken then has a word with the Couriers reporter for 5 minutes whilst I have a blether with Jim. Jim wants me and Ken to have oor photo taken together with us holding oor fists up each other's chins. Ken with a wee sparkle in his eye agrees, revenge will be sweet, as we stick one each other's chin getting harder with each punch. "Easy now lads" the photographer says, "Aye sure says Ken." From where we are standing, I could look down to the, Bells, sports centre where the teams were changing and see them heading of for the short walk to the pitch, "time to go Ken" I said.

We said our goodbyes to Jim and the photographers and headed down to Bells. As we approached, we saw an old friend sitting outside waiting for a couple of Fife players who were turning up late. "Hi Mig" we said. "Hi" he replied, and he asked where my brother and Marshall were. "Oh, they took off to a gala day along the coast" I replied. Ken sat down to chat with a lass, a barmaid from the east dock at Methil where the team from Fife drink out of, whilst I went in search of the late comers and found one of the coaching staff from the Fife team in the bar having a wee refreshment.

I went down and got both Mike and Ken and walked over to the pitch, the sun was out, and it was getting very hot, and here's Ken in a polo neck lol. The poor bugger will roast in no time. A photographer arrived to take both team photos as prearranged by Jim Mason. The game itself was very heated, this was going to be no friendly, with feet and hands everywhere. Still the end result was a good 4-1 for my team, Letham amateurs. Ken still thinks we are shit, "Aye I should have brought my boots and showed yis how it was done he says." The Buckhaven team manager says, if we play like that against East Vale FC we will get run over. Poor loser, aye sure we will. We in fact went through to Leven the next week and stuffed them 6-1 so, get it right up yi son.

As the teams were getting changed, me Mike and Ken had a drink in the restaurant before heading to our team's sponsors hotel. On arrival we had a pie and a couple of bottles of beer and then sat talking to the young lads in both teams. I am sure most of them are not aware who Ken is, and who by now is sweating for Scotland. One of the lads said he would get Ken a shirt from his house. "No, I'm fine" says Ken. Yeh right Ken. Come on, let's get to the nearest shop and get you a shirt. TK Max, 500 yards along the road looks good, and we are soon both rummaging amongst the shirts. Ken picks out a black light weight shirt, "This will do me Jock. "Right let's get it wrapped up and paid for" but Ken can't wait to change in the hotel, so he gets on with it right there in the shop foyer. "You look braw big man."

We have another couple of beers with the lads, leaving Kens old polo top at the bar to pick up later on. We then head of into town telling the lads we will meet up with them later, which we did. We go to a new bar in town, The Sandyman. It's a big building already filling up with customers, so we grab a seat and order a quick bite to eat. Ken has the steak whilst I have the usual hamburger with a bottle of beer and a glass of red wine for Ken. A big group of lads come over to speak to Ken, they are all from Edinburgh and have recognized one of their own. A great time is had by all, as we are really get stuck into the refreshments.

Mike is somewhere in the town drinking with his work colleagues. I try to get a hold of him but with no luck, which is strange as he normally likes oor company. Anyway, we do a wee tour of the town together before I get a call from one of the team, saying they are all in Dickens bar and that we should meet up. This was soon done, but bye this time it's getting late and we are both getting tired, it must have been the heat? We say goodbye to the lads and head out looking for a taxi. "What about my top" Ken asks. "We will pick it up tomorrow nae rush tonight eh" I replied. We sneak into the house because the wife's up early tomorrow for work. I rise early as normal and go for a wee walk for the papers. At about 12 o'clock I get the man up as time is marching on, two cups of coffee later we head into town to pick up the man's polo top. We have a good chat on the journey back to Kens place and arrive in good time. Glem looks very happy to see her wee men back after a good night oot. May there be many more. We give each other a big hug and I head back home reflecting on a good night, back to normal eh?

The Comedy Club, Perth 03/09/04

Not long after this, the wife and me took it upon ourselves to go on a wee holiday to Turkey, so on route to Glasgow airport we stopped off to see Glem and Ken. They were both in high spirits, so we sat for 30 minutes bletherin about nothing in particular, except for me giving Ken confirmation about a couple of jobs. I had arranged for Ken to attend the Glasgow rugby club in January and asked if he would like to come through to Perth for the opening of the Perth comedy club, hosted by Bruce Fummey, the comedian who worked at Kens night at the lodge in Scone. This was basically, to support Bruce in his new venture and sure enough Ken was up for it, plus I knew that Bruce had a lot of contacts through the after dinner speaking circuit, and that the papers would be there for the opening. I had also arranged for Ken to present Bruce with one of his caricatures. On return from my holiday in Turkey, I got a call from Ken saying that he has bought himself a wee car to get him around. "Great, I'll no have to pick you up on the 3rd for the opening of the comedy club then?" "No, I'll make my own way through for about 6 o'clock." "Great see you then." As normal Ken gets lost, in fact he stopped on Stormont road in Scone and asked a lad if he kent me?

His name was Derek Stewart Campbell, who worked in the gym alongside me in the regiment. Derek pointed Ken in the right direction. So, Ken knocks on the door, comes in, and I say, "Find the hoose nay bother eh?" "Aye easy" he says. I never did tell him about me knowing he met up with Derek lol. The Comedy Club gig wasn't that big, it was just a night out for ourselves. A good laugh and wee drink, then a few in the town then home. Just a good relaxing night, but like most nights with Ken it was over too soon but we had done our job in supporting a local artist trying to get by.

The Bomb Shell

Just when you think all is going well, up jumps something to kick you right in the nuts. It was about 9.30pm (30thAugust) when the phone goes. Its Ken and he is very upset. "Jock Glems dead." Through the tears and sobbing I made out that Ken went to wake her after an afternoon nap about 5 o clock, but she never responded. He felt for a pulse in both her wrist and neck but to no avail. He said he will make all the arrangements, funeral, lawyer etc and that he would keep me informed. I asked him if he wanted me through tonight or first thing tomorrow to help and lend some support? "No yir all right pal. Glems sister and brother are both close bye." He said his goodbyes whilst ah sat for a wee minute deep in thought before informing the wife.

The Bomb Shell

To think we saw her last week, where we took flowers and the four of us sat down and had coffee for a while before we headed off to Turkey. She looked fine then, fuck is life no fair, or what? I phoned Mike and let him in on the news and he just asked how Ken was. Well, me and Mike went through on the morning of the Funeral, as he had met Glem on a couple of occasions and like me wanted to show his support for Ken. In the house was Ken, his dad Tom, and another lodger John. Ken looked ok but was very noticeably quiet. Ken asked if someone else could drive his car as he didn't feel like driving, so Mike said he would drive. We all got in the car and headed to the area of Firhill, where we thought the service would take place. We are early so we popped into the first boozer where Ken announced that he had left his wallet in the house.

Not much was said about that eh. So, I got the drinks in. John the tenant sat down and started speaking, (he doesn't look all there I thought), "I'll just get myself a glass of whisky with this" he said to Ken. While he was at the bar Ken must have picked up on my look, "Jock he is a confirmed alcoholic," aye but are we no awe the same I thought. We had oor pint and headed off to the services. We sat in this wee room where we met Kens girl and his old manager Gerry. We sat for about five minutes before Glems relations started to head in. Glems sister looks like her double, but her man, George, looked a right card, a bit shifty if ye ask me. We were then taken into another wee room where we thought the services was going to be taken. After a wee while the funeral directors phone rang. He answered then said to all seated that the minister will not be joining us here but has asked me to say a few words on his behalf. I will say two poems after this then we will head out to Maryhill crematorium by procession where we will meet the minister. We all looked at each other and thought what a fuck up, this is no right, we never said a word though. We got back in oor car and followed the funeral car. It was a good wee drive and when we got there, we all sat together. Why was Ken not invited to sit at the front, he knew Glem better than all these hangers on. As Ken said, he has never met any of them until this time, not once did they bother to visit Glem, money grabbers?

I sat next to Kens dad then Ken, then his girl, Mike and Gerry with John sitting behind us. As the service was under way Ken was in tatters, his dad and lass holding his hand. I passed him a hankie, (homer Simpson playing football), and after the service we all stood up to leave. But not Ken, he would not get up. I left him sitting till last with his dad and lass at his side. What a sight, this hard, proud man in tatters, crying for an old lady he really, really loved. He will really miss her. Outside waiting was his big pal from his local, Tam. We pile into the cars and head out to where we think the wee reception would be, following Gerry. "The cunts lost" I say to Mike. We stop outside this pub where we see a couple of men with black suits and ties on. Me and Tom go in for a pee, Mike follows, whilst Ken and his lass wait at the bar.

I come out but don't recognize any of the lads standing at the bar, dressed as if they had all come out of a funeral parlour. Hi lads, are yis from the Mrs. Steel funeral. No were from the Mr.----------- funeral, fuck wrong funeral party. We even tried next door whilst I'm helping myself to the biscuits on the table and getting an eye full, from Mike. "What? I'm starving." "Nay respect" he says. We head out looking daft as fuck and go to another place someone had mentioned earlier, yip they are all here. Ken is no happy, they bastards sent us to the wrong place, deliberately, fuck them let's eat. We sit at a table that's not made up and order a pint and we speak to the family out of respect. what a shifty lot eh Mike? What a poor funeral, this has been not well organised, we are lucky in Perth.

Who gives a fuck when yir dead though I thought, as long as everyone gets a good drink and doesn't call you all the names under the sun? We stay for about 30 minutes before heading back to the cars. Gerry heads into Glasgow, Kens lass to her own house and the rest of us head back to Cumbernauld and the pub, Moriartys, not before stopping of at the flat to pick up Kens wallet. In the pub sits his big pal, his wife and another couple of people who know Ken very well, they are not a bad lot really. Me and Mike stay for a couple of pints, well Mike did, I was on the Irn Bru's, as I was driving back to Perth.

Along comes another bloody bombshell

Its Sunday morning 13 of September. I go for the morning papers and I sit down to read through the news of the world. Whose face is staring back at me? Yip its oor Ken. 'Boxer Ken in catfight' was the headline. On reading through the article, it says Glems sister and her man are having a go at Ken, that he is a bum, punch drunk and has lost the plot, you get the picture. Ken is quoted as saying those bastards are no throwing me oot of my flat, Glem left me paper work saying I can stay here for as long as I want, so fuck them. I take it the reporter got Ken after a night on the sauce.

So, I phoned the hoose and after what seems like an hour, Ken says "Aye who is it." "Fuck me do you no sound rough" I said. "Oh, hi Jock, how are you." "Aye, sound a lot better than you." "I'm feeding the cats he says." "Got the papers yet" I ask. "No what's the matter." I explain. "Bastards" he says, "fuck them all, money grabbing bastards." then he breaks down. "Oh Jock, what am I going to do?" "Right, for a start you can stop greeting, don't you dare lie down to this shit, fight back. You have never given up and you're not going to start just because of this shit, get your arse up those stairs have a shower, get some grub in yi and get oot. Don't sit in feeling sorry for yourself." "Ok fuck them, yip that's what I'll do, yir a good pal Jock, yir like a brother to me." "Brother, if I was there now, I would be kicking yir arse. Lol." "Now get a grip and

Monday sees you back in the saddle. Get into your diary, you have a couple of jobs coming up and you can't let anyone down." "Aye I'll do that Jock, cheers pal. "I'll phone you in a couple of days to see how you are" I said, and we said our goodbyes.

I'm right on the phone to his Welsh brother minutes later explaining to him Kens wee development and ask him to give him a wee moral boost later on. Phil is a very good pal to Ken and has him doon at Wales later in November at a big civic reception. He also tells me not to tell Ken, but he has got him the only belt missing out of his collection, The Ring Magazine Belt, presented to those who have excelled in the sport of boxing, at his cost £1,000. He said he will phone Ken, he is good that way, and always worries about his Scottish brother. The story goes on and on and the next day I catch him in the house, "Well how are you today" I ask? "I'm ok pal, how are you?" "Fine, did you find that paperwork you said Glem had signed stating that you could stay in the flat as long as you wanted to?" "No?" Long pause. "What do you mean no Ken, you need that to stay in the flat." "I have got it somewhere I'm just no sure where about" He says. "Find it, get it photocopied and get it to your solicitor." I give him an ear full, he said he will stay aff the swally (off the drink) and get his heed together. Ken has been on the swally since Glem died, poor man doesn't know what way to turn. I phone him the next week and ask

"How are you pal?" "Oh, fine just sitting watching a couple of videos. I haven't had a drink for a week now." "That's great news pal. You have done all your greeting and mourning, Glem would want you to get back in the saddle."

Re-opening of two pubs

"Any way I have a wee proposal for you. I know you said that you are attending the opening of the Scottish parliament and then heading back into Glasgow for the Scottish Boxing hall of fame after it, but what have you got on the night before?" "Nothing how?" "Greg Keenan who has Tay bank Tavernier's would like you to re-open a bar at Inveralmond, just outside Perth. It will only take you an hour then drive to Carnoustie to re-open a bar there.

You will get £300 in your hand for your trouble." "Seems like a lot of fucking about for not a lot of cash" he says. "Piss off, do you know how long the man on the street has to work for that amount of cash?" "No?" "Anyway, it will give you spending money for your long day on the Saturday, don't knock work Ken?" "Aye yir right ok I'll do it." "You can stay at mine rather than travel back to Cumbernauld that night and the next morning you can have a shower and breakfast before heading to the capital." "Sounds ok, let's do it" he says. We say our goodbyes and I phone Greg to say it's on and start making a couple of posters to promote both openings.

I had been trying for a couple of days before the pub openings to get a hold of our Ken, just to ensure all is ok. Can I get him, can I hell? The day of the opening he phones me. "Hi Jock, how are you." "How am I?" I say, "where the hell have you been?" "I'm here now" he says. "Aye ok, are you still up for the opening of the two pubs?" "Aye sure." "Right be at my house for 1 o'clock and I will explain the short programme for the day/night." "Ok pal, see you then." I am out at the car when he arrives right on time. "Did you get lost?" "No, no much" he says. I get him into the house for a wee coffee before we head into Perth and theirs a message on the answer machine. 'Hi Jock, I'm at the Wheel Inn, where do I go from there?' Aye, you never got lost much did you Ken?

We have our brew then head into Perth, park up my car and head for the bank as Ken has to get some money out. I had previously explained all the details of the day/night. "Where are we going now" he asks, "Ken I told you we are doing a wee interview with the Herald and Post," a local paper that is not long out. "Oh, aye he says." We meet the lad that is doing the interview over another coffee, then it's outside for a photo shoot and Ken is in top form. All the office is hanging onto every story he is telling when we get back inside, it was a good laugh. About an hour later we are heading for something to eat, "Yip The Ring o Bells looks good" I say." "Fine by me too" says Ken. What a feast we had, and I pick up the tab. "Oh you should not have done that" Ken says, aye sure Ken.

We do a wee bit of shopping then head back to the house to chill out before heading to work. We arrive at the Almondbank Inn right on time. On heading into the pub, we chat to Jim Mason from the evening paper, who informs us that the hostage, Ken Bigley, has been killed by his captives, bastards we think out aloud. The pub is bouncing when we walk in. Ken hunts out the new manager and hands over the signed frame of 50 years in boxing, which I had organised for him. The manager is over the moon and soon the belts are out, and all the locals are wearing them. Oh, I forgot to say Mike our pal had arrived as well, looking smart as a bean but with a good wee drink in him, still he is fine. Soon the local papers are taking all the photos while I take some to test out my new digital camera. It's braw, with both me and Ken are on the soft drinks and Mike, well he is on the pints lucky bugger. Greg Keenan the manager who asked me to organise Kens visit is very happy with the way things are going, so, he heads of too Carnoustie, our next destination.

After about 20 minutes I said were leaving, to the applause of the whole pub and with the words of "Don't be a stranger" from the new manager ringing in our ears. We jump in the car and head Northeast. Ken is sitting in front with Mike shouting in the back, aye shouting as he can't speak without raising his voice when he gets on the piss, again lucky bugger. What a journey that was. I will be in no hurry to get back out there that's for sure, it doesn't help when Mike clamps both hands over my eyes and asks how I am? Crazy shit. We park close to the pub, the Arran Bar, and walk into a large room that looks bloody empty. "This looks good" I say. Greg is there and comes over and asks what we are drinking, same again we say. We sit down and take a good look around. "It will be ok Jock, it's still early for the locals?" Fuck me its past 8 o'clock already. Mike and me normally have 6 in by now.

We take a seat and 20 minutes later the room is filling up. The Karaoke man, Allan, is handing out song sheets. I speak with Greg and get Kens fee from him. He is chuffed with the response and he asks me up to the stage and tells me that when it is full, I have to introduce Ken to the attendance. Oh, cheers Greg. "Yeh fine no problem" I say, and here's me on soft drink. So, there's me up speaking for Fife, telling all the locals that it was Kens wish to come here tonight, to meet the supporters of the Junior cup winners.

Re-opening of two pubs

They just love this and are up looking to get their photo taken wearing the belts that me and Ken are tying on them. The locals loved it and I give Ken and Mike the nod, time to go lads. We say our goodbyes and drive back to Perth. Mike is still loud and when we stop in Dundee for Mike to have a wee pee, I start the car up and start moving away. "What are you doing" asks Ken. "leaving the noisy bugger here." "Yi cannie day that." "Listening to him is breaking my ear drums." "No dinnae day that" Ken insists. So, I wait for Mike to jump back in the car and as we drive of, I say "Mike, Ken wanted me to drive of and leave you." "You little lying shit, it was him Mike no me" Ken shouts.

So, an argument starts whilst I have a wee laugh to myself, couple of easy buggers to wind up lol. We drop Mike off at Duffy's bar in Bridgend, and me and Ken head back to my house, so he can get his keys and head back to Cumbernauld. He tries to hand me some money. "Don't you fucking dare" I say as I head him out the door. He hugs me goodbye and takes about five attempts to reverse out our we cul-de-sac. What a shit driver, any way a good time was has by all.

Round 7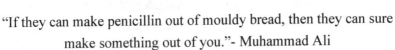

"If they can make penicillin out of mouldy bread, then they can sure make something out of you."- Muhammad Ali

Boxing weekend. 12-15 November

Before this weekend, the middle of November, I had spoken with oor welsh brother Phil Jones. He had told me about the big Civic Reception that has been planned for Ken on his visit down to Merthyr Tydfil. Ken didn't know it, but he was getting presented the Ring Magazine belt for his world title bout all those years ago, and that Carmen Basilio (the former Welterweight & Middleweight champion of the world and inductee of the international boxing hall of fame, the man who beat Sugar ray Robertson) would be flying over especially to present it to him. Anyway, back to the weekend I had planned for the 12-15th November. On the Friday evening Ken made it through to my house, but not without the normal phone call for directions.

He was in casual gear and as normal in no rush to get changed. "Wait till yi see what I got presented with at Wales" he said. He was like a wee boy with a new toy, and so he should be he deserved it. He takes his overnight case upstairs then heads straight back down holding a plastic bag and then takes out a beautiful belt. "What do yi think of that then" he says. "Great Ken, it's really nice." He then hands me his own programme from his civic dinner in Merthyr. "I'll go and get changed." "Aye sure

Ken." I sit down and have a quick squint through the programme. I never knew it, but Ken is the only British fighter ever to win the Edward J Neil Trophy for the American fighter of the year, which he won in 1970. You learn something new every day eh?

We set out for the boxing show In Kinross, with me driving and I explain the plan for the weekend. I deliberately don't go in to too much detail, as I know Ken will forget any way. Both boxing shows are to be held in Kinross and both run by Andy Caulfield who puts on a great night of boxing. Dick McTaggart and Frank Henry will be with Ken at the top table for both shows and both will be staying at the venue. Ken was given this option as well, but I turned it down for I thought that it would not be good for him. The first show was billed as a Scotland v England event.

It was a very, very good night which seen us departing at about three in the morning. It took me ages to get Ken out the hotel, not that it was his fault, because so many people wanted to spend time with him, take photos, autographs etc. Andy kept saying remember and bring him here on Sunday and if you want, he can stay here with us, we will make sure he is ok. "No thanks Andy I'll look after him." "Aye and you do that well too Jock" as he hands me an envelope with Kens fee and expenses in it. He shakes oor hands, gives us a cuddle and says in my ear "Don't forget Jock he means a lot to us," "Aye it will be fine nae problem." Ken talks about everything on the way back, his girl who he adores, people who he would like to smack fuck out off, aye he is in good form considering the amount of red wine he had put away.

We sneak into the house, as the wife is up at 6am for work and aye, I am taking her with less than three hours sleep, that's one you owe me Ken. Next day, I get him up at about 11 o'clock for breakfast and the first

Boxing weekend. 12-15 November

thing he asks is "Well, what's on the programme to day Jock?" So, I delight in telling him the initial plan. "Well, a game of football up at Alyth watching my amateurs." "Fuck its freezing, can we no go." "No, we will go" I tell him with a chuckle. We phone Mike to ask him his plans and see if he wants to come with us, but he is playing golf, the sissy. So we head north early, something I do a lot. (Hurry up and wait, it's an army thing).

On route, whilst chatting away, Ken asks if he can have some music on? "Of course," I say. "You can have the radio or a CD" and I hand him a bundle of my CD's to look through. As we are going along, I look in my mirror to see a flash of something hitting the ground from my car? Then a second flash, was that the sun hitting of my CD,s? Ken has the window open, saying out loud, "Shit, shit, shit," as he throws the CD's that he doesn't like out the window lol. It was too funny not to laugh but I tell him, this is going to cost you a lot of money to replace that lot. Aye right, he says, and he soon has Neil Diamond blaring out as he sings along to the tunes. This will not be the last time Neil Diamond is on as loud as possible with a good car sing song going on.

We get into Alyth early, park up the car and track down a café. It's a nice wee café, full of Brick-a-Brack etc. It was like having breakfast in an antique shop, and the lady in the shop was really nice. We sit and have oor bacon roll and coffee, then say a big thank you and head for the park. The lads arrive, 19 of them, so a great turn out, but the weather was bloody Freezing. The old lads watching the game with us are amazed that they are watching an amateur game next to a sporting legend.

The game as we expected up here is hard, they breed them tough up this end of the world, but we are holding our own and by half time we are winning 3-1. Keep our shape and discipline, and we will take away three points. By this time, me and Ken have had about three Bovril's each and with only 5 minutes to go it's still us in the lead, then they get a penalty. They score and now the score is 4-3 with one minute to go. As the scorer goes to get the ball out the net, our goalie has a mad turn as thumps him, all hell breaks out and both are sent off. Time to keep the head but no, our goalie (fittzie) runs after the lad that was sent off with him and they both start fighting outside the changing rooms. The spectators join in and soon both teams join in. The ref turns to us and says, "Right that's it, game abandoned. The replay will be later in the month." Fuck me, we have to come back up here to a hostile environment. Fergie the manager goes daft. He really gets stuck into the players, especially the goalie. Ken smiles and says, "Was it football, no boxing, we were here to see" lol. "Yeh right let's go and have a pint." "Good idea."

We park the car up outside the Lodge and have a blether with the lads, as old Jock arrives with his taxi and drops us of at Duffy's. Mike phones. "Where are yi?" So, we tell him, and we join up and head for a Chinese, for something to eat. I hate Chinese food but to keep the peace I go with them, and Mike is foo of drink and him and Ken share a bottle of red wine whilst I stick to beer. Christ is Mike no loud. After the meal Mike and Ken both argue about the bill, me I stand back no wanting to interfere, (yip that's the Fifer in me). We take in a couple of more pubs before heading back to Duffy's, who have a live band on called Face to Face. They are bloody good too. The place is jumping as I manage to get us a couple of stools, and we have a great night. Mike is up dancing with everyone whilst me and Ken watch his antics with a laugh, he is some man. I would like Mike to find himself a nice woman, one who would look after him. But time passes and we say goodbye and leave him dancing to himself on the dance floor. The wife wakes me up at about 6am on the Sunday morning. "You were meant to pick me up from work last night and to take me to work this morning. I will have to take a taxi now" she says. Stop shouting woman I have a sair heed, which of course I say to myself not wanting to make matters worse. I have a long lie in till about 12 and get up and make me and Ken Coffee and toast. "So, what are we doing today and tonight" Ken says. "Back to Kinross for a Scotland v Australia boxing show" I reply. "Oh right" he says, reading the papers, not really interested I thought. Right big man, upstairs and get ready. "Have ye got an iron, I need a shirt pressed" he says?" "You get in the shower and I will press it" I reply and with a smile he heads off, fucking mugged again.

I drive to Kinross. On stepping into the hotel, I meet up with an old pal, Paddy Reilly, a great lad. We have a wee blether as Ken speaks to the promoter and organizer, Andy Caulfield. Ken heads off to see Dick and Frank, so I hold on to the belts, whilst I speak with Paddy. Andy puts his arm round me and says, "Cheers pal it is very much appreciated." "Nay bother just don't forget the envelope" I reply with a smile, which I know he would never do. As this was an afternoon show things go quickly and before we know it, the show which again was first class, is almost over. But not before Ken tells me that he wants half of his fee to go to the exhibition bout, a good bout between two wee lads. During the interval we were introduced to a lad from the Kelty lodge who would like Ken to speak at a sportsman's night. Ken said "Aye nae bother" without even asking a date etc. I take the lad to one side, give him my card and say, "If you are serious, phone me and I will arrange it." Also, during the day, I spoke with another old BW lad who knew my brother better, Soapy Sutherland. He asked if it would be ok for Ken to come back to Leslie with them to their local, The Station Hotel. "Let me see how thinks look later and I will do my best" I say.

Before we know it, two of Soapys pals are in the car and we are heading oot to Leslie. They must have phoned ahead to say who was on the way to the hotel because we arrived to a great reception. All the locals took to the man and he was in good form. We must have stayed for about an hour and thirty minutes and the lads said, this will be the talk of this Fife village for years to come, how the great Ken Buchanan dropped in for a pint. We picked up the wife at work, I could not let her down again or my ears would get a real bashing, and to be honest I could have done with a pint, but nae chance now. So, sitting in the house with coffee, Ken speaks away drunk, no? Just full of life, he speaks away to my mum, brother, and sister. "Time for bed Noddy" I said as I'm working in the morning, early. This was a good sports week end, though shame about the football. Still a good time was had by all. Andy Caulfield phoned me up a couple of days afterword's to say a big thank you. He will go far in the world of Scottish boxing,

Dundee, Lochee sports bar

Ken phoned about two weeks before this wee night in Dundee to ask if I would accompany him. "Aye nae bother, you can stay over if you have a pint or if it goes on till late." "Cheers" he says. "It's a guy named Davie Martin, he had something to do with Raith Rovers football club a wee while ago" he continued. "There is no much money in it, but I will take a few prints if you will help me sell them?" "Aye sure" I replied. The day arrives. I remember the day, as this is when the snow fell in buckets into Perth and beyond. I phoned Ken later that day from Dundee to say that the roads are no too bad, but try and get here a wee bit earlier than usual. I arrived home from work to find Kens car abandoned outside the house. He says it was parked (my arse). Ken is sitting in the front room with a cup of tea and blethering to the wife. "Oh, hi Jock, how are you?" he says, "Aye fine and you?" "Braw, are you going like that" he asks?

I look at him as if he had two heads. "What, are you mad, you told me to wear a suit, no my working kit, (at this time I'm working for the court in Dundee). Christine says, "Mine and Kens tea is on, I'll put an omelette on for you if you want." "Aye sure" I say, as I head out the door for a shower. We have our tea and head out to Dundee in slow time as the roads are no bad, but I will rather be late in this world than be early into the next one. We arrive and park up just along the road from the evening's venue, as we were going to Frank Henrys bar for a quick pint beforehand. Just as we are locking the car up, Davie Martin is on the scene. "Hi lads, your early" he says. We explain what we were planning. He says, "I wouldn't bother Frank is never in his pub." So instead, we head straight to Davies pub early. We take up a seat in the wee lounge whilst our host gets Ken a Shandy and me a coke. Ken starts talking to a couple of old boxers who recognise him straight away.

I busy myself by looking at the sports photos on the wall and the place is soon filling up. Davie, our host, is directing the audience through to the function room. I meet a work colleague, Bernie, and his son who are big boxing fans. "You're on in two minutes lads" Davie says. "Yip we are ready" I say. Davie introduces Ken to the awaiting audience, and they all stand up and applaud him. That's always a good start. This evening is a question and answer affair and it is controlled by our host, who is very sharp and very well in control. Ken is very sharp and answers as always with honesty and with a lot of humour, in good form and after about 15 minutes there is a wee break, to refill glasses and get to the toilet. Me and Ken go back to the wee lounge for a soft drink and as we sit down the local press arrive. I get some of the lads together with a belt on, for the photos. Before we know it it's time for the second half off the night. The questions go on for about another 15 minutes and this I feel is Kens strong bit, then it's on to selling Kens prints and then more photos. This goes very well, and money is being taken hand over fist.

By now the time is getting on, it's about 11pm so, I direct Ken to one side and tell him it's time to head back. "Yeh no problem" he says, and we say our goodbyes which takes about 20 minutes. They all want a last photo or autograph and Ken doesn't disappoint, he never could. We head back knackered as that was a very busy night. Ken then says, "What's the big rush Jock?" "I'm looking to get a quick pint in Duffy's before it closes" I reply. "Nay chance he says" and he is right, its closed as we drive past. Ken stays the night and heads home some time the next morning, whilst I head of to work early. Still another good wee paying night for my pal.

Burns night 29th January 2005

I have been organizing this for months with the estate manager of the above club who stays in Scone, Colin Williamson. A nice guy who is very professional at what he does. Ken is happy with the arrangements, which I had sent him and his fee, so it's on then. It is going to be a wee bit different in that we are all going to do some work this time, not just Ken. Mike doing a wee toast, me doing a toast and a dressy up poem, and Ken doing his speech. A week before the function I give Mike the poem he has to do, (only four lines), no problem to a man who has stood up at a number of football functions, so he told me. It's not quit the same, I say but still, it keeps him part of the team, or as Ken says the three amigos. The weekend arrives all is in place, timings, dress, etc.

I pick up Mike early, about 9.30am and head out west to pick up Ken at the bus terminal at Cumbernauld. On route, me and Mike speak about the new love in his live, he is some lad. We spot Ken waiting as we arranged. He is wearing that bloody hat. A gentleman's hat is the way Ken describes it and we head for Airdrie so that I can see my granddaughter for a wee while. We get to my son's house and after about 10 minutes, Mo, that's Stuarts lass, shows Ken how to put names into his phone. I take photos of the bairn and we all have coffee, but we don't stay too long as I have a feeling it is going to be one of those journeys. Right Milngavie, here we come. To cut a long story short I have to phone the lass that is running the B+B at least three times for directions but she is giving us directions for the wrong road. Mike has his Mr. angry head on, and we argue, whilst Ken just sings into the end of his tie.

We arrive to meet the landlady and start organizing our self's, to get to the rugby club, as we are running about 10 minutes late. I hate being late, but Colin is very good about it and says no rush when I phone him. Mike asks the landlady if she wouldn't mind driving us, no bother she says, great lass. Waiting outside the club house is Colin and the club president and another gentleman. After introductions, we head up to the club bar for refreshments. It's a really nice club and two beers later we are directed through to the club's restaurant for dinner. It was a really, really good meal. We wine and dine on the full hospitality package and after the meal it's time to watch the rugby. The West are playing a team from Edinburgh, so Ken in his true sportsman's manner shouts for them? Mike is over the moon because his name is on the match programme, and when his name with ours is mentioned on the tannoy system at half time, he is well made up. The game is won in the favour of the west 24-14, so it's back to the club house for more refreshments. We are certainly getting well looked after. It's getting on, so I get the lads to say their farewells and climb into a taxi which Colin had ordered, to get showered and into suits for the evening.

Mike is first in the shower and he takes his time as normal. Why am I sharing a room with him again I thought, he snores and sleeps naked? I have nae luck. So, with ten minutes until we have to leave, I go up to Kens room to see how he is getting on. He has his room upside down, "I huv lost my bow tie he shouts." Just the news you want to here, eh. "Don't panic I say we will find it." Eh nope, he has forgot it, so it's back to the landlady, Irene, to ask if she has one, we can have a loan of.

She hasn't but will get a loan aff her son, who lives around the corner. What a lifesaver. The taxi number we have on the card doesn't want to answer, so it's back to our reserve, Irene, the land lady to beg a lift. Again, it's no a problem, but before leaving we all have our photo taken, and of course we could not leave Irene out, as she has been so good to us. Anyway, game on.

We arrive in time and are taken straight to the president's lounge reception, to meet other guests. Bonus, three former British Lions rugby players join us not just for a pint but also for the whole evening, great. We are piped into the hall, and Mike and me peel off to our table whilst Ken gets his seat at the top table. It's a 5-course meal, and it was excellent, then there is a 15-minute comfort break after which we return to our seats.

I am first on to do a wee toast to Robert Burns, after this its Mikes turn. He is nervous but gets through it, then there is 10 minutes of singing and piping, whilst I head out to get changed to do my poem, Such a Parcel of Rogues in a Nation. I come into loud applause and see a pint on the first table and go to take a sip. Wrong move, as at the table are all the young rugby players who encourage me by way of shouting "Down, down, down." I couldn't say no, so I downed it in a oner, that's the belly full now I thought. I get into my poem, then spies another pint belonging to the coach. I just pick it up and start drinking, fuck its Guinness. I look over to my own table, but all the British Lions lads have their drinks under the table. Mike had warned them off, shit.

A few lines more, then it's time for another drink. I'll take the Ministers brew. I'll be ok this time. Oh, shit its Gin, what the hell, I have it in my hand now. I finish my poem and head back to get changed. Coming towards me is one of the players who has a pint of Lager in hand and he says "Well done wee man, that was braw, here's a pint to yi." Cheers, I thought, just what I need. I say thanks and take a drink, down the toilet it went. Next its Kens turn, his first words are, thank Christ, I thought you had forgot about me. He stands up to a very good ovation, he is on form and gives the troops what they wanted, a legend in good form.

Yip this was one of his best 25-30 minutes of sheer greatness and the crowd were eating out of his hand. Ken finishes with his presentation to both the president and the estates manager and a large print to the club from the three of us. After a couple of rugby poems, we were presented with a club tie each, they were very loud, but braw. The next step has us back at the bar for more photos and with plenty of banter from our guests.

Burns night 29th January 2005

The British Lions lads are great fun regaling old stories about the English, but we don't overstay our welcome and head for a taxi at a reasonable time of about 1.30 in the morning. Good lads, so we are back at the B+B and I put on the TV and fall asleep? Mike goes to investigate a conversation up in Kens rooms direction. Its Ken, standing in his jammys with his belts laid out on his bed, together with the next room's guests, who are English. He was showing them the belts one by one and they were amazed, so Mike recalls.

My sister gives me an early call at 7.30 in the morning. Good lass, "Get up yi wee bugger, I am returning the favour as you phoned me at 12:30 last night, drunk." Christ I'm always doing that, and I quickly remember. "Have a good night did we?" "Aye sure, I'll phone yi later byeeeee" I reply.

At about 9am, Mike and me get sorted for the day. Mike is up showering and after about 20 minutes he appears. "Big toilets them he says?" Strange lad, he even took a picture of one before we left? What was all that about, he must have really been impressed, as I take my turn in the toilet. I ask Mike to get the man up. As we enter the breakfast room, there are four other guests enjoying their breakfast. We soon get into the swing of things. So yir English are yi, I think's to myself. We pour our self's milk for our cereal, its goat's milk we're told. "Is that so, that will do us fine" we say. We sat and enjoyed a really good breakfast as well as entertaining, through good banter, our old enemy. Actually, they weren't that bad, and as they got up to leave the lassie's says "Do you mind if we take our milk? " lol.

There is other milk in the jug, but we had been using their own milk, "Oh sorry" we said, "We thought it went with the breakfast. After breakfast we pack the car, but before leaving we all chipped in for a good tip for the lassie of the house, plus, Ken left her a signed print and we had her photos taken with Ken and all the belts. We said our goodbyes and headed back home. Just as we left the road heading to Cumbernauld, I said to Ken "You did remember and square her up for the rooms, didn't you?" I asked. Instant panic in the man's face "Oh shit no, we will have to turn back that's rotten." We let him rant on for a wee bit before letting him in the secret which is I paid for the three of us.

On the route home Ken and Mike wanted a hair of the dog but not till I get rid of the car first as I want one too. So, we drive past Cumbernauld and head straight for Mikes house in Perth. He collects his stuff and says I'll no be a minute. Five minutes pass. I phone his mobile. "Where the fuck are yi?" "I am on the pan, I couldn't wait." "Well snip it and get oot here, we are looking for a pint." Out he comes muttering, "I wasn't finished" he says. So, straight to my house, to quickly of load our cases etc. Mike disappears into the toilet. "I'll have to finish this" he says. I phone a taxi, which will be about 15 minutes, so I ask them to tell the driver to pick us up at the Old Drome / Kinnairds pub.

We walk down after Mike decides to get out my bog and we just get a bottle in hand when the taxi pulls up. "He can wait" I say. Mike goes out to explain our case. Mike returns and downs his in a oner, I am a bit slower and Ken doesn't even finish his. We head down to Duffy's for about 3 bottles and Karen, behind the bar, is a great laugh and we enjoy the banter. After about two or three pubs later Mikes new lass, joins us. Mike drops her off at a pub with a pal whilst we go for an Italian meal next to Mikes flat. After not a bad meal Mike returns to his lass whilst me and Ken do another three pubs, before heading back to the Drome, for a last drink.

We stagger up the road to the house and at the door I remind Ken about how I was supposed to have picked the wife up after her work. "Aye but you sent her a taxi and you paid for it." "Do you really think that will soften the blow, nae chance." We got the ear bashing we deserved but it would have been better if Ken wasn't laughing like a banshee, so I joined in. Fuck did we no get it fast and furious. When she was finished, she sent us both to bed like wee laddies, thank Christ she was away back to work before we got up.

I drove Ken back to his house that afternoon and as I dropped him of he gave me a big cuddle and said thanks for a great weekend, no thank you pal.

Save Scottish Regiments Dinner, Perth

It was around about march of 2005 when I spoke with an Anne McMillan who was one of the organizers of the above Dinner /Ball asking me if Ken would lend his support to the event. I said that he was a big supporter of the Black Watch, as he has in the past done Burns suppers, presenting trophies at boxing nights and even recruiting for them in Dundee. So, I would ask him and find out what his plans were that evening? Ken was of course up for it, so I asked two good pals from my local amateur football team, Bob and Fergie, if they would like to come along as Ken and my guest for the evening. (tickets being sold at £34 per head). Yip they were up for it. They both enjoy a good night out and the both know Ken as well. So, I can't wait till Saturday the 12th of March?

The night before the function I get a phone call from Anne McMillan the organizer. "Jock, do you and your lads mind sitting beside Scott's dad and pal? (Scott Harrison the W.B.O. champion). "Not at all as long as they put their hand in their pocket" I replied. Long pause. "That's ok then, thanks." I had to drive to Cumbernauld about 9:30 on the Saturday morning to collect ken, as his car is off the road. I get into his new road but could I remember the number? I try him on his mobile, it's turned off, shit, I see a postie. "Hi pal, it's a long shot but do you know where Ken Buchanan now stays?" "Aye number 119, I spoke to him this morning going for his paper." (does everyone on the planet know Ken I thought?). I knock at the door as he is picking up his post. "Oh, hi Jock, see you found it ok." "Aye nae bother, first time (lie), no like you Ken."

He collects his stuff and we head out to the wee car park. "Right Ken, out of all these cars what one is mine?" "Oh, that's easy he says it's the big black one?" "How do you know that" I ask. "Yir driving and parking is shit." Cheers pal. We start to head north, and he is impressed with the new wheels. We stop at the Stirling services for a wee cup of tea and a chat as time is on our side. He speaks about a wee job he did for a pal, selling double glazing, he seems good at it. We drive straight to the Drome for a quick pint. Well you have to, don't you?

Arriving at the house Ken has a quick chat with Christine as I lug his belts up to his room. "Mind yir warm coat Ken, its Baltic at the fitbaw" says Christine. It takes us 5 minutes to arrive at the park and Ken sits in the car whilst I warm the players up. Its bloody freezing and after about ten minutes into the Game Ken arrives. We are playing shit and Ken is soon on hand to explain why. "The coach must be pish" he says. "Ken, that's me" I say. "Aye I was right then." Halfway through the game I spot Ken wearing a pair of tracksuit bottoms wrapped around his head. Fuck, if only I could get a photo I thought, but unfortunately, I had left my camera in the house.

Save Scottish Regiments Dinner, Perth

The game finishes 2-2, which was a fair result. Fergie said, "Well Ken you still haven't seen oor team beaten yet", and he was right. Back home to get changed but first the wife had made something to eat, well she told me what to cook is more to the point, but it was for me and Ken anyway. Ken is in the shower after me. Once he is finished, he says, "Jock can you come up a minute?" "Aye what is it?" "Two things, one I can't turn off the shower." So, I show him, "Next." "Look at the shower head, a piece has fell off, is it supposed to?" "No Ken, but don't say anything, we might get away with it." We are soon changed and I'm on the phone for a taxi. "Yir going early are yi no" the wife says? "No, we are meeting Fergie and Bob in the pub before the function" I tell her.

So, we hit a wee bar before meeting up with the lads and it's full of Welsh lads up for the rugby. "Your pal looks very much like the former world champion" he says in a broad welsh accent. "Aye he does eh?" His pal says, "shit it is he." Before you can say I'll have a beer out comes the camera phones. Ken is soon signing pieces of paper etc. He is also speaking to brothers and fathers of the Welsh lads on the phone. Oor Welsh cousins are really good lads and are soon getting the beer in. Fergie and Bob step into this mayhem and are soon joining us at the bar.

I check out the time and remind the lads it's time to go. As we walk down the street, Ken reminds me how cold it is in every swear word he knows. We march into the Salutation hotel and go straight into the bar where yet again we meet more Welsh lads, who immediately recognize the man. I leave him and the lads to get the beer in whilst I speak to a local newspaper photographer, who I get to take the lads photo with a piper etc. (it turned out well the next day). Anne McMillan the organizer soon tracks us down, so I introduce her to my company. We stay that long at the bar, we are in fact the last to get to our table. Ken had introduced me to Colin Joneses brother and we took our seats, introducing ourselves to those at the table, with Peter Harrison and his friends plus a very nice couple. Peter was in the R.A.F. regiment. We bought raffle tickets etc. and had a great meal and a good few glasses of wine. Peter in fact bought Fergie a bottle and they seemed to get on very well. The former head of the Scottish prison service and an old colonel from my depot days had a word with us. A great lad, Brigadier Clive Fairweather, he is a real man's man.

When Alex Salmond, the S.N.P. (Scottish National Party) leader arrived, he shook my hand. I told him he was late and had missed his starter, but he was on good form and wanted his photo taken with Ken later. "Aye only if you have one with the lads as well." "Aye nae bother" he said.

Kens framed print went for £210 in the auction. We stayed talking for what seemed ages at the table and there was speeches, raffles and auctions all going on, it was a great night. I am sure both the lads had a great night. Peter Cruickshanks and his pal popped in later to say hallo, he is a good lad, and more photos were taken. We soon found ourselves back in the bar and in with the welsh lads. Fergie was having a great time of it, as he said there was people here who knew his family. Ken was soon looking rough, so I said I would phone a taxi. I had just got back from the phone when he says, "Is it no here yet?" No, you are right Ken it's no? After about 6 more attempts to get him a taxi we decide to wait outside and take our chances. It worked as we said we were someone else when the taxi drew up and headed North to Scone, well it was 2:30am ish. A great time was had by all. The wife and me took him home the next day and then on to Airdrie to see our beautiful granddaughter, and her mum and dad.

Round 8

"My arms are too short to box with God."

- Johnny Cash

Downfield Jnrs Dundee 24th March 2005

It was through Andy Walker that I got the call for Ken to travel to Dundee and do a wee question and answer night, with the Downfield Jnrs football team. We were to meet him at the Little Chef, just off the Kingsway duel carriageway, at about 19:15pm as we did not know how to get to the evening's venue. We had both met Andy when Ken was last in Dundee. The arrangements were for Ken to arrive at my house for about 6:30pm then on to meet Andy. I have had to arrange for cover as I am on the night shift in my new Job (Reliance custodial services). I have had to also pop into the town and sort out a frame for a print, as I am sure there will be a raffle at the club. If not, I'll keep it for another event.

Ken phoned me to say that he was on his way, Early. He arrived with a youngish lad called Derrick who turned out to be a nice lad. He told me he drinks with Ken and always referred to him as 'Champ' and has a lot of respect and time for him. After a quick Coffee, we took Kens car, then we headed to the pub as I did say we were early and for a change I was not driving.

We were in plenty of time, meeting Andy where we had arranged, and he jumped in to oor car and gave Ken directions to the venue. Ken had us about off the road on a number of occasions, I am sure I have said before he is a shit driver. Anyway, we arrive and get directed into a wee back lounge for a drink whilst the punters start to take their seats. It's a really nice big club and after about two pints and a lot of blethering, Ken is given a good introduction, then its game on. Me and Derek sit together near the bar and near the man at work.

Ken has the attendance of about 60 eating out of his hands, he is doing well, and then there is a short break of about 10 minutes, before the second set of question and answers. Ken also does the raffle which consisted of items that Ken had signed, gloves, boxing tops, etc. then it's down to photos and selling prints. This goes very well and by this time me and Derrick had sunk a few, well done the driver. I pull Ken to one side and slip him his money for the night and what was made on the prints. I had previously asked Derrick to count it all and Ken tries to give me a wee back hander, but as usual I give him a mouth full and walk away. "You don't give away your wages Ken" was the last note I left him with. We say our goodbyes and Andy gives us another date to think about, as we drop him off on route, before heading back to Perth for last orders in the toon. Then it's a final goodbye, as they drop me off at the house after another good night.

Kinross Boxing show, 6th April 2005

Andy Caulfield, the coach from Kinross Boxing club, phoned me up a wee while ago to ask if Ken would be ok to attend one of his International nights? As normal I asked for the date and the venue, and phoned Ken to ask if he was not booked already. The date was ok by him. It was to be a Scotland Select v Ireland Select boxing match. Ken was to collect a token fee and bring along one of his Edinburgh prints, as Andy had a frame (for the auction) and of course bring along his belts. The usual suspects would be in attendance, i.e. Frank Hendry, Thom Brown, Dick McTaggart and a boxing promoter. Ken had previously informed me that he had just attended a course on Kitchen fitting with Mobil, down South and seemed excited about the prospect of working a steady job, at the same time, getting away to do his Boxing speaking engagements.

Well its 6pm on the night of the show and Ken is no here? Late? Well it's not unusual. By 7pm, I ring Andy Caulfield, the nights organizer, to say we are running late, i.e. Ken is not here yet. He asked me to keep him informed. Ken does not show and after phoning his new local, I am informed that he had been out drinking that afternoon. So that will be that then, I thought. He phones me the next day whilst I am out visiting Mike. "Sorry pal about last night, I have been on the drink" he says. "That's ok Ken, but you must phone me to say you are ok as I was worried about you" I replied. "Sorry brother" he says, and when I get home I find he has left two messages on my phone saying sorry.

Glenrothes Show, Sunday 20th May 2005

I get a call from Ken saying that he is on a wee bender and that he would like me to accompany him to a show, to be held in the Pinkerton hotel in Glenrothes. It's organised by Steve McGuire, who we have both done work within the past, but in fact it was a few years ago now. Anyway, he said he would be at the house after he has picked up his belts from his lassies place, but he could not give me a time. He then asks me what time it all starts, cheeky bugger? It was him that organised this gig? Anyway that's 12:15pm and he is still no here, then the phone rings. "Jock I'm a wee bit lost." Now there's a shock, "Where are yi?" "Ah dinnie ken, I am lost." I just happen to look out the back window and see him sitting in his car, which is parked on the road at the back of our house lol. I nip out and get him, "I wasn't that far out," he says? We have a coffee and discuss the arrangements for the gig, but Ken is a bit unsure. Ok, "What time do we have to be at the venue Ken?" I ask. "No sure" he says. "What are you getting paid." Again he says, "No sure, but Steve said he would see me ok." So, we have something to eat, have a good wee blether and we head out the door about 6 pm. The venue is only about 30 minutes away so that should be early enough.

We arrive are in good time as I thought we would. Ken as normal is signing gloves, programmes etc. for all the young lads & lassies. We are then both ushered to our seats by Steve who is happy to meet up with Ken again. As I said, they had done a few shows together before. Ken has his belts with him, and all the young kids are trying them on. I am trying to keep an eye on them but it's like herding cattle, lol.

The show gets underway and it's a good one, with the young boxers battling two different colours of crap out of each other. They are no holding back, lol, and it's a pretty decent standard of boxing as well. During the interval, there is the usual raffle, heads & tales games etc. and then Ken is asked to get in the ring and say a few words. As usual, he is in good form and soon has the audience laughing away. During the evening, Steve squares Ken away with his fee for attending. We then leave the show during the last bout to get back up the road, as its pishing it down with rain. On the way back Ken is trying to give me money. "What the hell are you doing?" I shout. "It's for petrol etc" Ken says. "Bugger off" I reply, "you did the work tonight, but you can get the drinks in the pub when we get back hame." "Aye ok, that's fine with me" Ken replies. We are soon blethering about the show, having a good laugh and singing out loud to Neil diamond on the CD player, which we both like.

After parking the car at my local pub, Kinnears Inn, we nip in for a couple of pints, it would be a shame not to lol. Anyway, Alex and Catherine who run the pub enjoy Kens company, so a wee lock in is on the cards, but only for couple of hours. We leave the pub well-oiled and on the way back home we walk through the local park. I say to Ken "Give me a minute, I need a pee" and nip I into a bush. Ken does the same and as we leave the bush, pulling up our zips and blethering away, we walk right into a nearby police car lol. The occupants had seen us coming out the bush together and with a wry smile on their faces they say, "All right lads? Had a good night?" Ken says, "Aye great, how (why)" (he was never a fan of the lads in blue). As we are walking away, Ken asks "Jock, do they think we were a couple of gay lads coming oot the bushes?" "Nah Ken, just a couple of happy drunks" I say, lol.

So, next morning I am sitting downstairs having a brew, when I hear some commotion coming from upstairs. After a wee while down walks the bold Ken in his boxers, he looks surprised? "What are you doing here he says?" "Ken, I stay here, this is ma hoos." "Oh aye, so it is." He sits down and says, "I thought that was you in yir bed, in the room next to mine." "What have you done" I ask. "Oh nothing" came the reply. The wife comes down with a look of fizz on her face. Do you and Ken no want a cooked breakfast" she asks? "Eh no, we are ok" I say. Ken hides his face in the paper, but I am sure he is laughing lol. The next day, the wife had told me about ken climbing on oor bed and jumping up and down shouting, "Get up yeh lazy bastard," obviously thinking it was me in the bed. Now that's funny lol, what a man. Ken then drives back to Coatbridge after what was another eventful night in his company. lol.

Lodge Minto Lochgelly, 28th May 2006

I was sitting in the house on the morning of the above function when the organizer phoned and asked me if everything was ok for the night. "Aye, no bother it's all in hand" I assured him. It was, everything was arranged, but I was knackered as I had just come of night shift choked with a cold. Bruce Fummey, the comedian, had not long phoned to ask me directions to the venue but I didn't have a clue. Kens lass, Gully, had phoned to ask what time Ken has to be at my house for? He had went out and got hammered and ended up at Gully's that evening and was in a shit way, not my words but hers. "He can't drive Jock, not in the condition he is in." "No problem I will pick him up" I say. "All that way, no, I'll drive him to your house. What has he to bring" she asks? I gave her a quick rundown and went and phoned Mike to pass on the information, and approx. timings. He is fine with this and like me, has been down this road before. Gully and Ken arrive after a couple of phone calls. Christ what a state yir in Ken I said to myself, but I shut my face and told him yir looking no too bad. You'll be fine and we jump into my car and head down to Mikes, after dropping the wife off in the town.

We get a mile or two outside Perth when Ken gets me to stop. I pull over on to the hard shoulder where he is sick and boy, was he no sick, pure water it was. Next stop, Legends lounge in Dunfermline to pick up a signed Dunfermline FC strip donated by Jim Leishman, what a braw wee club. Ken has an orange juice and Mike and me have a pint. Ken looks a wee bit better and after stopping to get my photo taken with him outside, we drive the short distance to the B and B where the women of the house was very nice. Ken is freezing, so I put an extra duvet on his bed for his return and Mike gets his own room. The organizers young lad picks us up and takes us to the venue, only stopping to pick up another guest on route, a young lad (Mike I think). We have a good laugh, mostly at his expense but he takes it in good form, and we are dropped off at the local pub, just across the road from the lodge.

Raymond Wilson, the organizer, meets us at the door and we go into the pub where I meet up with an old pal, Jock Gilfillan, who is to be the MC for the night. I introduce him to both Ken and Mike, and we all have a pint and chat away. Ken is looking brighter, as we head over to the lodge and have a quick chat about the nights programme. Ken and Mike head for the bar to meet the other two speakers, whilst I go outside to go over my own wee bit, "Grace." Back inside I have a quick word with Bruce the comedian, and Willie Anderson, a former Scottish international rugby player, then we take to our seats. Mike is still at the bar and he returns with his arms full. A bottle of Bacardi, 6 cans of coke and a pint of ice cubes, he is looking to settle down for the night, I think.

The top table is piped in, after which the piper takes a seat next to us. Jock the MC gets up and introduces me to say grace, which I do without messing it up. The nights going well. First, it's the turn of the rugby man, but it's no rugby stories he does but jokes. I look over to Bruce who looks pissed off, as this is his area for the night. Then its Kens turn, and he is in good form doing all the normal stories, then its Bruce who still looks pissed off but gets on with it, a true professional. There is a drunk sitting being an arse so Bruce fires back at him, but he is getting out of hand and his pals are not even trying to shut him up.

Bruce says fuck it and sits down not happy. He says. "The drunk cunt should have been flung oot on his ear." Both me and Mike speak to him afterword's to pacify him and say forget it. He laughs, gets squared up and leaves as we head to the bar and Mike gets another bottle of Bacardi. After we had sunk the first one, I get 4 bottles of beer. We had won 20 beers in the raffle but decide to keep them for another night. Raymond squares me up with Kens money, then we head outside to find a taxi after being told there is no bus organised to get us home. Nay luck though as everyone's looking out for one and it's also boxing time outside with lads scrapping in all directions, so we head back into the lodge, stepping around the bodies as we go. Raymond's young lad is phoned and comes and picks us up, good lad, and in no time we are back at the B and B. Its bedtime now. I cough all night so, Ken the next morning gets his own back by getting us all up nice and early, easy seeing who wasn't on the juice eh?

He goes for the papers but returns empty handed as the garage is not open, so he sits and speaks to me. I'm still in a trance having no slept with coughing all night and Mike is the last to surface. We square the women of the house up and head out to the Glasgow road where both Ken and Mike know exactly where they are going? Yeh right lol. "Shut the fuck up both of yis and let me aim the car, myself" I says. We get to Kens none the worse and we say our goodbyes. I decide to go and see my granddaughter, son and girl in Airdrie.

Mikes Golf Clubs

Ken gives me a wee call. "Hi Jock, I have moved." "Oh aye, where to this time" I ask? "Leith Walk, Edinburgh." "Great" I say (at least he is out of Cumbernauld). "Ken what are you doing next weekend." "Nothing, why, what's on." "Me and Mike are going oot on the Friday night, to his golf club Craigie hill, and there is a pal of mine who would like you to visit his dad who is a big fan of yours, but he is very ill." "Aye nae problem, I'll do it." "Right, be at my house for 7:30pm." "Nay problem" he says. Friday arrives, it's 7:40pm and no sign of the man. Ten to one he is lost yet again I say to myself, so I give him a phone. "Hi Ken, where are you", "I'm turning in to Scone now, will be with you in 5 minutes." Yip, you guessed it, 5 minutes comes and goes. So, I am ootside looking up the road he should be coming down, but there's nae sign of him. Next thing this car draws up next to me, its Ken, "Did ye get lost?" "Nah" he says. Aye right.

He pulls in to oor drive whilst I stop to talk to Dell Campbell, a sergeant from the same regiment I was in, who is posted (Army term for being assigned to another barracks/Unit/Location) to Perth. He says, "Do you know that man getting oot the car." "Aye" I replied, "He is an old pal of mine." "Is it no the boxer Ken Buchanan" he says. "Aye yir right." "Do you know, he asked me for directions to yours about 10 minutes ago up the other end of the village." (Naw, you never got lost did yi Ken?). Ken puts his overnight stuff into his room, and we have a wee chat. Something like, "That car Ken, it's no the one you had the last time you were here." "Naw, I gave that heap away to a pal in Cumbernauld and got this one, good eh?" It was. He writes a wee note for the wife, the creep, he has only went and got her a box of chocolates. I give Mike a call and say we are on our way. Ken takes his car as he is not drinking, and we pick Mike up and head to his golf club. On route Ken tells us about this doing (beating) he got from two police officers in Cumbernauld, where they split his head, broke one of his fingers, and turned him over. What a way to treat a sporting legend eh? Ken said he is getting done for being drunk and disorderly.

But he said he was ok. He said that the police noticed who he was and decided to go for him. Anyway, he is going to sue them as the hospital took photos of his injuries. He was also supposed to turn up for my brothers 50th birthday party at Methil, but as he said he has been on the drink for a wee while. However, he did send a nice wee present inscribed no less, and he phoned him the next day.

PKAVS fund raiser

"Hi Ken, are you doing anything on the 9th of September?" "Naw" he replied. "What about doing a wee job at the Perth and Kinross voluntary service fun raising dinner?" "Aye I could." "It's a cash in hand job, I will send you on all the details nearer to hand." "Aye that's fine with me Jock you sort it all out yirsel." So, the details were duly sent out along with Kirsty's wedding invitation. It's a couple of weeks before the function and Ken has not rung to say he got what I had sent? Then the phone goes. "Hi ya Jock, how are you" the man says. "Oh, fine how about you." "Aye ok, I'm at Gwen's, are we still ok for the Saturday?" "No, it's on a Friday night pal" I said. "Oh, aye sure it is, do you want me to bring along a framed print?" "Aye Ken, we already said this." "Oh aye." "Ken, I have a good frame. You bring one of your Edinburgh prints and we will sort it out when you get here, I am off the whole day so if you can get through in the afternoon it would help." "Aye nae bother, my car is getting fixed." "Ken, any problems with the car and I will pick you up if you want"? "Nah it will be all right." "Nay bother. I will give you a wee bell before

Friday ok." "Aye sure, say a big hallo to yir wife." "Aye and you tell Gwen I said hi."

Friday comes along, I take a day off work and Ken gives me a call saying there are road works just outside Perth. He says that he will be with me in about 10 minutes and 30 minutes later he appears. I don't say a word, I'm just glad that he has turned up. We have a quick chat then he shows me photos of his 60th bash with Mark, Gwen and his dad. He has a look at the print I said I had, (he had forgotten to bring a frame), but he did have a print which he leaves with me, to be used at a future date. I phone a taxi. He gives me a shout "Jock I have forgotten to bring cuff links, got any?" "Aye here. I got these of a good pal at work, Brian Raitte, after you gave him that boxing glove a wee while ago" I says. But he has forgotten all about it. Not to worry he looks sharp and as the taxi arrives, we head out.

We arrive at the beautiful Hunting Tower Hotel which has got to be one of the best hotels in the whole of Perthshire. We are met by Gordon, the lad I spoke to too arrange for Ken to attend. We are handed a glass of Champagne and led into the main room to view all the great items which were to bea. A Peli top, Ali photo, Kylie Minogue CD disc and many photos and lots of other items, which will no doubt go for thousands. We were introduced to a number of other people, all terribly nice, it was very, very posh. We went into the bar and just spoke to each other, then Ken was ushered out into the foyer to meet Mrs. M Grey and get his photo taken with her for the papers. I even spoke with her and got my photo taken with her by Ken, which he thought was a good laugh, as Muriel stands at least a foot taller than me. Ken was to be sitting at the main table and I sat next to Jim Mason, Jim from the Clan Alba association and four young lads who were very, very good company. They really enjoyed their drink, the meal was nice and posh, and we helped our self to the free wine. When that was finished, I started on the bottles of beer with the young lads.

After the meal the main speaker, Muriel Gray, got up and spoke. The lassie produced a no bad speech as she spoke about her life and stuff. Ken was then introduced and did about 20 minutes of his normal speech which went down very well, after which the chairman joined him and got on with the auction. It was a great auction, raising a lot of money for their Association, but Ken looked bored, this is not what he is used to, he likes sportsman's dinners etc. Still you can only take what you can get and after it was all finished, as usual, a lot of the guests wanted their photo taken with Ken.

We stayed for a wee while longer, then I got a hold of Gordon to square me up for Ken. We went into a wee bar area where he counted it out, he shook my hand, and said a big thank you for Kens work. Ken shook about a hundred hands before we got to the foyer to phone for a taxi. When it arrived, It was my good pal, Andy Lothian, who was behind the wheel. We also gave the chef and his pal a lift into town, and after dropping them of we went home. Andy wouldn't take anything in the way of a fare, and as we walked to the house, I asked Ken what he had done with the belts. "Fuck, I have left them in the taxi, (we were of course missing Mike who normal looks after them). I rush into the house and phone the hotel to get Andy to return to the house not mentioning what we had left in his cab.

Andy is soon back at the house and Ken thanks him and tries to hand him some money. Andy is still unaware what we had left and as I fish out the belts, Andy clicks, and asks if he could see them. "Aye nae bother" the man says, in fact try them on. So, we have a wee fashion parade outside the hose, it must be about 2:30 in the morning by now. (My next door neighbour reminded me of the time the next time she saw me, was that no good of her?). Andy is over the moon whilst me and Ken are just relieved.

We get in the house both still wide awake, so I hand Ken a beer and we sit and chat for a while. Ken takes his plate tooth out as he said it was annoying him and I remind him no to lose it. "No, I'll no Jock." Guess what happens, he phones me the next day as I am at work. "Jock I have lost my plate, av had a good look for it everywhere but canny find it." "I'll have a look when I get home" I told him, but unfortunately, I couldn't find it. However, Ken found it in his suit pocket a couple of weeks later.

Ken In Hospital (2)

My phone goes about 2:30 in the afternoon but I don't answer it as I'm on the night shift and when I eventually get up, I find out it was Kens lassie, Gwen, who had called. She left a message, "Jock can you please give me a call." So, I phoned thinking, no doubt Ken is in the shite again. "Have you heard about Kens accident Jock? He jumped out of a first floor window, as he was hallucinating about some people trying to get at him and broke his ankle. He phoned me whilst still lying in the street. I told him to phone Mark as he lives just round the corner, which he did, and he is now in the Royal Edinburgh hospital. I am going to visit him today with his dad, can you pay him a visit as he would like to see you?" "Sure" I said, "I'm on the night shift but I will phone the hospital and find out the visiting times."

Ken In Hospital (2)

"Mike its Jock, what are you doing tomorrow, Sunday?" "Why what's up?" "Kens in hospital, I will explain on route." "Ok, I have told Lewis I will look after the wee man." "That's ok, if you can get the car seat we can take him with us for a run." "Aye fine, we will do that then." It's 2 o'clock in the afternoon, and the three of us are off to Edinburgh, the wee man is a joy as he is never any bother, he just sits and laughs.

We arrive about 3:30 and go looking for ward 109, nae bother. It's a beautiful hospital, well laid out, and we find Ken lying in bed, mask on, hooked up to a machine, with his dad Tommy sitting passionately beside him. A bloody sad sight to see. "Oh, hi Jock, hi Mike, hallo wee man," he says. "How is he Tommy" I ask. "Well he had his operation this morning, and they have had to put a plate in his ankle," he says, "To think what he has done and know look at him lying there." He starts to well up. I put an arm around his proud shoulders and say, "He will be fine, it looks worse than it is." Ken is in and out of consciousness, as Mike says he is still under the effects of the drugs from the operation, again he is right.

Mike takes the wee man down the stairs to the foyer, whilst Ken lies sleeping and me and Tommy step out his room for a wee chat. We discuss what will happen when he eventfully gets out. "He can stay at my house" Tommy says, "As there are no steps to climb up and down." "Aye, I'm sure that's for the best" I say, but I would like someone to come in from the medical side and speak with him, regarding getting off the drink. He must want to do it himself and he can when he wants too. We speak for about 30 minutes and go back in. Ken is awake and is just lying looking at us both. He reaches for a bottle to pee in and Tommy asks me to help him. I pull the curtains to give him privacy and ask him to try and turn on to his good side, holding both him and the bottle as he has his pee.

Nothing like taken the piss eh lol? I hold the blankets up for him as he sorts himself out and Ken and his dad start talking about his assault by the police. A letter has been sent to his old address by the police. Both Ken and Tommy are still bitter about the incident and so they should be, two police officers beat up an old man, very brave of them eh. After about 5 more minutes I have to say goodbye, as I am still on the nightshift and have to get back to Perth.

Tommy thanks me for the visit, Ken says thanks as well and to Mike and the wee man. And to think I thought he never was aware they were there. He wasn't that out of it then? Did he hear what me and his dad were saying about him, any way he will get better and he will sort the police out for doing him over, albeit in court. Look out the police complaints committee. I tie up with Mike and the wee man and head back to Perth, a Scottish sporting hero lies in an Edinburgh hospital, and no one is any the wiser, I hope it stays like that. Get well soon pal.

It's been two weeks since me and Mike took his grandson to see Ken, and do you know what? I later read in both the Sun and the Record newspapers that Ken is in hospital with an injury, which may prevent him from attending the Sparta's 60 years in boxing event. Also, both papers said Ken was 50 years old, he wishes lol. So, during this time I have been trying to get a hold of Ken on his mobile, but it just goes to voice mail, so I phone Glem, his lassie, and she phones me back. She is down in England working but she said yes Ken is still in hospital but a different one from the one we visited, so she gave me the number. I phoned and a nurse said that Ken was in good spirits but does not want to speak with anyone? I think I will pay him a wee visit when I am next off work.

Ken In Hospital (2)

Well, I find myself heading off alone to the Astley Ainslie Hospital in the Grange area of Edinburgh. I was given directions by the nurses when I phoned up to ask about visiting times. It's not easy to get to they say, to bloody right it wasn't. I seemed to be going round in circles for ages. Then I got into their grounds which is in a big area with lots of small wards. On entering Kens ward, (Mears Ward), I was told by the nurses that Ken was in fact sleeping. No for long I said to myself, and after accidentally knocking into his bed he woke up. "Oh, hi ya Jock, how are you?"

We sit for an hour just speaking about the accident. He can't remember me and Mike and his grandson visiting him. Just as well after me taking the piss out of him lol. I ask him if he has been out for fresh air at all. "Nah, I huvny been oot the door." "Right, we will soon change that, you need to get some fresh air into you."

I get a hold of a wheelchair, Ken gets a warm top on, a nurse gives him a blanket and we head off to the W.R.V.S. coffee shop. We sit and chat for another 30 minutes or so, then head back to the ward. The others on the all-male ward seem nice but strange. Ken told me about a talk he had with one of the doctors, asking him all sorts of questions for 3 hours. They were trying to find out if I was nuts or something, he told me. "I am fine Jock, but I have to keep oot the pub it's going to kill me." Twenty minutes later I'm on my way back home, lost again looking for the bypass, after saying a sad farewell to my pal, poor cunt he looks so lonely. I phoned the hospital a good bit after this. I was feeling a little guilty as it was in Perth that Ken had his last working night out.

It was about a week later, aye, it was the Thursday before the Sparta's 60 years in boxing, when I got to speak to the man himself. "Jock I have

142

found one of my diaries and it says I had to speak to you reference a show at the start of January." "Ken, that was two years ago, you me and Mike went and did this." "Oh, aye ok, Jock I'm going to the Sparta's night. Do you know that Bruno is getting £7,000, his flight accommodation etc. all paid for and I'm getting nothing?" "What? What does Bruno know about the Sparta or in fact Scottish boxing, it's your old club not his" I said. "Aye, I Ken Jock, I am trying to get a hold of the organiser to see if he will give me some money up front."

I remind Ken of another date he may have forgotten about, an amateur international in Kinross. I said he will get paid up front and asked if he can get Mark, his son, to get him to the venue. "No, I will get Mark to come to your house then bring you back" he said. "No that would mean at least 4 journeys for him. No, if I go, I will meet you at the venue, but I will tie all this up after talking to Andy Caulfield." I replied. "Aye that will be fine Jock." "Right Ken, you look after yourself and have a good night at the Sparta show." (I wish I was going with him).

Afterwards, he said the show was ok but left early as he wasn't feeling to good. He is staying with his dad at the moment due to him not to clever on his feet yet. His dad Tom had a ground floor house so it will make it easier for him getting about. I phoned Andy Caulfield about a week before his boxing show. "Hi Andy, how are you?" "Not too good, I have a rotten cold" he said. "Sorry to hear that pal, just thought I would ring regarding timings for your show for Ken?" "Did I say Ken was invited" he replied. "Aye sure you did; you spoke to me in Perth city centre a wee while ago." "Oh Aye, but I never heard from Ken after he failed to turn up for my last show and I was really let down" he reminded me. "Andy, I spoke to you on why Ken was not able to attend, he was sick." "Aye well, I'm still no to happy he let me down." "Ok Andy fine, I'll phone him and pass on your concerns." Down goes the phone, rotten shit, I am thinking. Well he will wait a good wee while before Ken attends another of his shows that's for sure. I phone Ken and pass on what Andy had said. "That's ok Jock, it doesn't matter." But in his voice, he sounds unhappy, I feel he wanted a wee outing to get him oot the house.

More Photos

Me, Duran and Ken

Glasgow Function

Me, Ken, Bruce, Derrik and John (Magic)

Me & Eddie Avoth

Ken, Me and Paul Appleby

The Ringside Doctor and Me, the Timekeeper.

Me and Ken

Ken, Margaret & Greg Keenan, Me
(N Cyprus)

Me addressing the Scottish ex Boxers association, looking
for sponsors for my Sahara Desert trek.

Russia, Trek Mount Elbrus. (Dae ye like the Kilt lol.)

Me in PPE with Ken, 19th Aug 2020

Round 9

"Never Fight ugly people—they have nothing to Lose."
- "Irish" Wayne Kelly

Leith Walk, Edinburgh

I had phoned Ken about a wee job I wanted him to do, it was in fact a speech at my son's wedding, on the 8th April, but I never told him about it until we had arranged to meet up. So, I asked the wife is she wanted a wee hurl (drive) through to Edinburgh to do some shopping for an outfit for her son's wedding. No, I'll go another day with your sister. Fine then I'll go myself, I feel a plan in the making. I get through the Edinburgh traffic at about 11am, that is after giving Ken a phone to say I was on route and was I on the right road, but no reply. So, I find a no bad place to park and head out on Leith walk to find the flat. I find it ok but none of the downstairs buzzers work, so I head to the nearest boozer as you do, not far, just next to the flat.

That's handy I thought, as I order my pint and take in the surroundings. There are photos of Hibs (Hibernian Football Club) players all over, so I take it it's a Hibs bar. I give Ken a phone. "Where are you" he says. "In your local bar having a pint" I says. "That's nice he says, look up at the flat I can see you." I look up and so he can. "Get yir arse down here, you were meant to be meeting me" I say. "It's no my fault it was Jimmies, I couldn't find my phone" came the reply. Five minutes later in walks Ken and all the regulars say hi Champ. "Did I leave my stick in here last night" he asks? "No Ken" says the barman. "Want a pint Ken" I ask. "Aye sure, anyway how are you and how's the wife." "All fine" I say. "That's nice." "Right Ken lets have this pint then go up to the flat and talk business." "Aye sure nae bother" he says. After about 15 minutes banter with all the locals, me and Ken head to the flat.

The stairs to the flat are very steep with a real old tenement look to the place. Ken lets us both in and Jimmy Pace, who owns the flat, is sitting watching T.V. Ken introduces me. It's a nice flat and Jimmy excuses himself as he can see me and Ken want to talk. "Right Ken, first things first, can you sign this photo for one of the lads in the regiment." "Aye no bother Jock." "Right Ken, I would like you as an old family friend to say a wee toast at Stuarts wedding to welcome his wife Moira into the Mcinnes clan. I have taken the liberty of putting down a few lines about each member of the clan." I pass him a wee brown envelope. "What's this" he asks?" "Every job I get for you, you get paid in cash so, this is your payment for this wee job."

"Aye and that will be fucking right, I'll dae it for nothing" he says really offended. He continues "Christ, I have slept in his room mare times than he has in the last few years, nut fuck of." I knew this was all coming. We have argued about money before, mostly when he has been trying to give me some form of payment for getting him work. "Right let's look at it from a different direction" I says. Here goes spin, spin and more spin, you need to get to the wedding, you don't have a car, you will need accommodation for yourself and yir bird, and a few bob in yir pocket to buy me drink. "Bugger of Jock, nae chance."

Leith Walk, Edinburgh

Jimmy comes into the room to ask if we are both ok? We give him a wee smile, and he about turns smiling. "Put it in your pocket and let's talk about it after" I say. "Right only if we go 50/50." "We'll see. Ken says "I have something for a wedding present." "But you are already giving them £200 for the drinks on the table" I remind him. "Aye, but this is nice, they will like it." We go into Kens room. He says, "This has been under my bed for about 6 years." My imagination is working overtime now. He pulls out a brown suitcase and opens it with a wee key. Inside is a 70-piece cutlery set. "What do you think of this Jock." "It's great, they will love it" I say. "No Jock, just look at each piece." Fuck me it's stamped 23-24 carat gold, it's fucking priceless. "Ok Ken" I say. "I will accept this, on behalf of Stuart and Moira if you give up, kicking up about not taken the envelope." "Aye, but just for now. Right, with this settled let's go for a pint" he says. "But I have the car Ken. "Fuck it, is it parked up safely" he asks? "Aye." "Well let's get Jimmy and head up town.

However, Jimmy declines our offer as he has too much to do, stripping paper off a wall etc. So, me and Ken are soon outside hailing down a taxi. We stop outside the Last Order pub. It's a kind of beefeater gastro food pub and it is full up. I can see people staring at Ken as if to say, is that the tartan legend? Ken gets the pints in, and we find a wee table and look through the menu. "Where do yi pay he asks?" "Fuck knows" I say "but I will go and ask at the bar." His phone goes, I leave him to answer his phone, and go to order. Just my luck, you can order at the bar and pay for it. I got £20 off the wife before I came oot, still when its gone its gone eh? On my return a smartly dressed man is asking Ken for his autograph for his sons. Ken say "That was Owen Smith on the phone something is going on with Alex Arthur. He's a tight lad, he'll no pay for anything but I'll tell you about it after." (He never did get around to it).

"Where were you going the other day when I phoned you Ken" I asked, "were you at the airport?" "Oh aye, I was going down to London to Joe Pyle's birthday party, but I got way laid at the bar." (Joe was a major player in the notorious London underworld of the 1960s,)

We had our meal and a pint, then we head out into the beautiful sunshine that has taken over the capital, down into the famous Rose Street and into the first of many bars that day. Not that our aim was to get hammered, just that we like to talk in bars. Seems fair to me. We had done the whole of the bars in the street, except the ones that looked garish, and then it was up the west end, then a taxi to the top of Leith walk, where Ken knows everyone or is it that everyone knows him? Any way the banter is great, as is the foaming ale.

On route home Ken takes me in to an Italian restaurant for something to eat, he knows the manager he says, and he did. Ken orders a half bottle of red wine for himself and me a half bottle of white, as he knows that red gives me the bouk (sick feeling). The meal was first class and we head back into, believe it or not, Kens local, the first bar I had walked into much, much earlier in the day. Ken starts talking, shouting and swearing on the phone to someone but I pay no attention. Then he passes me the phone. "It's yir wife asking how yir no coming hame?" And laugh's his head off. "Shit house" I say and start to back pedal my way out of it. I was going to phone her later. He gets the round in whilst I look sheepish, as if I have just had my ear bent, which I had. "Pint pal" he says. "Aye why no, in fact make it a Bacardi as well seen as ye phoned the wife." We are standing at the bar blethering, when Ken says that lassie is looking at you, "Do you ken her." "No, ah canny say I do." She comes over and is it no one of the wife's old army pals.

Just as well I am no talking to some other bird eh? We exchange old memories and say we will pass on our good wishes to each of our partners. She leaves, and we have another pint before heading home to Kens flat. I find my camera and start taking photos of us, fuck knows why, because it's there I suppose. Anyway, I wake up next morning feeling no too bad, but trying to recall the decoration in the room to get my bearings (i.e. where the fuck am I)? I remember the layout of the flat and head for the toilet, but on my return to the room I had left, I see another body in the bed. Its Ken fuck me.

Sharing a bed with Mike in Wales and noo Ken in Edinburgh, the wife will be getting worried I thought. After a wee while we get up and Jimmy makes us a cup of coffee and we sit and watch a boxing video for a good wee while. I then get washed and changed for my return trip home to Perth. I say my goodbyes to two good lads, and head out to the car with a 70 piece, 24 carat gold cutlery set under my arm. I hope no cunts looking. On my way home I am in a good mood, had great night on the swally and the wife is working, so I won't be getting my heed nipped until much later, braw.

The Son's Wedding

So, the wedding was to be held in Coatbridge. It started out real hellish weather, rain, followed by hail stones, and then snow, but an hour before the wedding the sun was out to split the trees. It was during this time Mike pulled me away from running around like a headless chicken, to say that he had got a phone call from Ken to say he will not be able to turn up. I was not going to let this spoil this day, so I took it in my stride, as I was sure that he would turn up. Gwen had phoned me to say she will be going to Glasgow Queens street train station to pick Ken up. I said that if he is not on the train, to still come through herself as she would be more than welcome. We had all just left the main hall after the ceremony, covering the happy couple in confetti, when up the wee slope to the hotel walks Ken and Gwen. Ken looked rough with Gwen helping him along with one hand, and his walking stick in the other.

I greeted him like a long-lost son. He had tears in his eyes as he knew he missed the wedding ceremony, but he was here. The family all came down to say there hallo's as did Stuart and his new wife Moira. As I had to get my photo taken, Ken and Gwen made their way to the bar with Mike in tow, he's a good lad. When I see him later, he was in good form chatting to the best man and his company. We were then asked to take our seats for the meal with Ken sitting next to Mike (planned). He was in great form now and stood up when asked to say a couple of nice thinks about the happy couple and the Mcinnes clan. After the meal he sat beside me and the family and he stayed for about two hours before saying his goodbyes to the family and Moira and Stuart. Two wee lads just had to get his autograph, and he also got a couple of photos taken with Stuart and Moira. Mike saw that he got to Gwen's car ok and Ken thanked me for the invitation, with a tear in his eye. I'm just happy to say that he turned up, it took a lot. In 20 or 30 years from now Stuart and Moira can say they had a legend at their wedding as their guest.

Cambusbarron, Sportsman's Dinner

I had been planning this sportsman's dinner for a good wee while. The top table guests were to be Tam Cowan, Murdo MacLeod and Ken, with Ken collecting a good cash return. Two days before the evening, the organizer phoned to say that tam Cowan had called off and that Gordon smith, ex Rangers player, would take his place. Ken made his way through by train to Perth that afternoon. I picked him up and went home for a quick cup of tea, before heading to the village local, for a Shandy. We soon headed off towards Stirling. We almost got lost a couple of times but soon found oor wee bed and breakfast. Ken was out the car first just to make sure we were at the right address. He spoke to the lady of the house, who took both our overnight bags and said she would drive us the short distance to the venue, braw.

We both got dropped off in plenty of time, with Ken stopping and joking with the lads outside having a fag. We were led into the main function hall to look at the top table and the seating, and also to sort out the framed prints we had brought, for the club and for the auction. First things first though, a pint with Ken sticking to Shandy, well he was working after all. After about ten or fifteen minutes the remainder arrived, we were both introduced, and then small talk took over.

After a short while the organizer took us through to a small waiting area so that the paying public and their guests could take their seats. When everything was settled down, the top table was piped into the hall with me holding a short respectable distance behind. They took their seats whilst I sat nearby at a table with three other lads. Soon the meal started to get served and I started getting some beer into me, with some strange looks coming from my table companions. "Why don't we all put in a few bob for the next round, I said" One of the lads piped up "Yir putting some drink away considering your Buchanan's driver?" "Fuck off, who told you that shit" I said in my politest voice? "I am his pal, no his bloody driver.

157

Me Fifty, Canny be Surely?

Aye sure enough, my fiftieth was just round the corner. My twin sister, Janet, like me did not want any fuss, just a meal with close friends and family. So, it was decided that we would have a meal, in The Burns Tavern, Kennoway. So, there was (if I can still remember) me, Janet, Jim, Sean, Kirsty, Brian (Tyson/Cameron) my mum, Christine's mum, Stuart, and Moira, Jim's brother and aunty, Brian's mum and dad, Mike "no show without him" and Ken. No, I haven't forgot my big brother Willie and Arleen his partner, it's just that he went out on the piss and never made it. (It was only my sister and I's 50th birthday meal after all!) Your right, I am still not happy about this unselfish move on his part. Ken said rather than me come and pick him up, or him making his way through to Perth, he would just get the train to Kirkcaldy, the nearest train station to Methil. So, on the day, me and Sean, that's my sister's son, went through to pick the man up.

His train was smack on time, and he was waiting at the station with case in hand, (why the big case? overseas here we come). Ken was looking very smart as usual. Sean jumped into the back of the car, as me and Ken caught up with gossip on the way back to my sisters, where we were all staying the night. The meal was very good and the company was great, I just wished my Bro would have been there. After the meal, we had a good few drinks in the Methil ex-serviceman's club, and the East Dock bar, where we met up with my bro. I am a happy man now. Willie P(rat) got a flight up from England along with his English pal Mike, then a taxi to his sisters flat, Helen in Methil. Willie and his pal slept on one mattress, but willie actually spent most of the night outside because the bingo was on. Helen loves her Bingo and Willie was trying to sober up (no change there then). Willie took a photo of us all at the club all leaning onto the banisters outside, all drunk, but hey it was my 50th lol.

Northern Cyprus

When my good friends Greg & Margaret moved to Northern Cyprus after selling out to Belhaven brewery, it was supposed to be to retire. However, the bug of business was never far away and the place they picked to retire too was still under a severe, and unjust in their opinion, United Nations Trade Embargo. As a result, Northern Cyprus has suffered economically and is a bit behind what we would call the economic norm, even coming from Scotland lol. The year was 2005 and people were driving around in Renault 9's (a French car from the 1980's) and a Renault Broadway was considered a luxury vehicle.

Greg saw a business opportunity, as there was little in the way of accommodation for holiday makers and visitors to the area. I got a call from Greg who said it would be great for Ken to come over to Cyprus and do some work for him. Aye but that's going to cost you pal I told him. He said he would give it some thought and I told him I look forward to hearing from him. A week later he gets a hold of me. "How about this, both you and Ken come out to Northern Cyprus for a five days stay at my hotel, on me as a wee holiday and I'll pay for the flights as well, all Ken has to do is do a wee bit of hospitality?" "Sounds ok to me pal, I will speak to Ken." I'm thinking to myself, game on lets pack.

The few hotels could usually only be found in the larger towns and tourism was not yet established, but more and more expats were buying villa's and apartments, and there was speculation that the country was beginning to open up to tourism. If that was true, then there was a need for them to have places to stay. This presented an opportunity and a challenge and Greg negotiated a lease on a very large old villa, that had been locked up for quite some time. It had seven bedrooms and lovely terraces. It could be turned into a boutique hotel and in time it was, but Greg wanted to make a splash with publicity and he contacted me asking if Ken and me would be interested in doing the opening ceremony. After coming to an agreement, the date was set and the local paper, the Cyprus Today, was informed.

This was a big event on the calendar for the people of Northern Cyprus, as they were not used to celebrities or famous people being in their midst back then. The day went extremely well and all the local dignitaries were in attendance, the Mayor, the police chief, the head teacher, the doctor, the Mukhtar (head man of the village) etc. Ken had brought all of his belts and he made time to pose with them for as many photographs as people wanted.

When we arrived at security at the Cyprus end, the security police person asked Ken what he had in his case? Ken duly opened the case and under his clothes was his 5 title belts? Minutes later all the staff had on belts and were posing with Ken. He even gave the police chief a boxing lesson. The paper did a big story on the visit and the hotel was launched, and a presentation was made by Ken and myself to Greg and Margaret, to mark the occasion. Not too long after our visit to Northern Cyprus and the printed newspaper article, another boxing star arrived to set up a training camp for an upcoming fight. We wonder if he had heard about us and our adventure, it was none other than David Haye.

Kens dad, Tommy, passed away

I got a call from Ken to say that his dad Tommy had passed away. He had been ill in hospital in Edinburgh for a good wee while. He was in fact

Kens dad, Tommy, passed away

97 years young and Ken was naturally upset, which got me going as I was very fond of the old man. I would phone him almost twice a month for a wee blether and catch up, recalling boxing down the years, talking about football, etc. He was Hibs oldest season ticket holder, a great old bloke. Anyway, as the days went on Ken phoned to say that the funeral was to be on Friday and asked if I make it. "I want you there with me, in the family car, and holding a cord at the grave side" he said. "It would be a great honour" I said and would be over the moon or words to that affect.

Then I thought bugger, I am working on the Saturday afternoon and can't get out of it due to others being off, so, I will just have to watch what I am drinking. Carol Ann said she will fix something out about sleeping arrangements. I said "Nae probs, I will sleep on the floor if need be."

So, it's now Friday and I am driving through to Edinburgh myself as my wife, Christine, is working early on the Saturday. That's a shame as I would have liked her to have been there, but a night drinking in Leith? Sure, I will get over it somehow. So, through I go and get there nice and early and park up the car in a side street not far from Carol Anne's. I get to the door, but looking at all the numbers on the close door has me thinking, what bloody number is it again? 1 forgot eh. So, I rang 3 numbers and some kind sole lets me in. I get up to the front door and give it a big knock. The door is opened by an older man in shirt & tie. "Hi, I am looking for Carol Anne's hoose." "Yiv fund it" came the reply. So, in I march whilst the man that opened the door disappears into the bedroom. Sitting in the front room is Mark, Kens son, Ken himself and Phil Jones, a great friend of Kens from Merthyr Tydfil in Wales. Honest, he is sound lad, he was with me and Ken when we first met up with Duran in

Kens dad, Tommy, passed away

Newcastle many years ago. He also wrote a wee book on Ken called The Adopted Legend. So, I give everyone a good wee cuddle and Carol Anne gets a wee kiss on the cheek whilst she is busy making sandwiches and coffee, before we depart for the service,

I can see that Ken is a wee bit upset, me I would be bloody raging as the man who opened up the door to me comes into the sitting room wearing white shoes and a black suit, to a funeral, what the hell must he be thinking? He looks like the stylish spiff, from the St Trinian's school film. So, were all sitting in the front room, not saying much and after a few minutes Carol Anne's daughter, Elizabeth, arrives. Introductions are done, then the car arrives. Ken is counting heads. "Fuck there's too many of us, the car only takes 6 and there is 7 of us" he says. "Not a problem Ken, if it's ok with Phil we will walk." "That would be great, it's only round the corner" Ken says.

So, Phil gets the directions and off we trot and 5 minutes later we arrive just as the car pulls up. We are ushered into a wee back room at the funeral parlour. I sit with Phil, whilst Ken, his brother and his son, Mark, take up the front seats. Raymond, his other son arrives and sits up the back with someone he knows. Jimmy Paste arrives, another sound bloke, who has known Ken for many a year, and he has a quick blether with me. Jimmy, me and Phil are stuck for a wee lift tae the graveside, so Ken says "Nay bother I'll sort it", and he did. Five of us squeeze into an old lads car, (many thanks for that by the way) and it's not too far to the Cemetery, only about 10 minutes away. The service was very nice and sad, but they all are aren't they.

We walk behind the car, following it slowly to the graveside. The undertaker asks for those who will be holding a cord to step forward. Kens lad, Mark, does the honour's and gets us up to the graveside in the right order and I notice Ken is not taking one. As I pass him, I ask him to take my place instead, but he says no, his eyes are awash with tears. (He said later on that if he had a cord, he would have let it go). So sad, so sad, as we lower Tommy's coffin. I look up to see my old pal break down.

Fuck this is so sad. The undertaker asks us to drop our cords into the grave, but I am not finished just yet. I throw my cord in a loop, so it gets caught on the side of the green felt carpet arrangement. Two supporting poles are put down, then a large board with the flowers on it is put down. The minister says another few words then the service is over. The congregation move to speak to the family, as I take the undertaker to one side and ask if he could cut me off a piece of cord (which I snagged). "No bother" he says, as he goes to get himself a wee knife. I take the wee bit of gold braided cord and slip it into my pocket. Phil has seen my move, so I explain to him what my plan is, which he thinks its brilliant.

After a short time, we all get into the cars and head to a local pub where the wake is to be held. Ken is holding it together, or so I thought. We have a couple of drinks in the local then Phil had to leave to get back to Wales. He is a cracking lad and a very good pal of both Ken and I. I took a couple of photos of both Kens sons, Mark and Raymond and after a short while they both left. I took Ken to one side and said, "Can I have a word pal?" "Aye sure what's up" he asked." "Ken, you never wanted to take a cord, and yes I fully understand why, so, I took the liberty of cutting a piece of cord and putting it in my pocket." I handed it to him saying "Ken you never ever have to let this cord go. It's a wee keep sake, a memory." He took me in his arms and gave me one hell of a big cuddle and through tears said, "Thanks bro, its much appreciated." I think Carol

Kens dad, Tommy, passed away

Anne put it in her bag for safe keeping. Carol Anne, Allan, Kens brother and myself, then headed just out of Leith to a local pub for a meal. It all started out ok, but tensions were high for some reason.

Ken was having some words with Allan about their dad's house, money etc. As it was none of my business, I tried to pass it off as a couple of brother's letting off steam after a very Emotional day, but their voice's got louder and louder until it went into a full-fledged fight. Ken told Allan to make himself scarce before he went mad and Alan quickly left. So now there was just the three off us, but not for long. Ken was still blazing mad, and Carol Anne tried to tell him to "Keep the heed," advice which only fell on deaf ears. So, after a couple of loud exchanges Carol Anne left, with her parting shot, "You'll no be staying at mine the night." Fuck, I said to myself, that was where I was kipping too.

So just Ken and me left then? Well nothing for it but to have another drink which then turned into a pub crawl. Ken was throwing them down like no one's business, even the nips in one pub, where there was a lassie singing. I got up and bought a couple of beers. Ken, as quick as a flash, went up and got himself a nip (whisky), then decided to sit at a table himself. I thought ok I'd give him a few minutes to himself and then go over and have a word, but in hindsight I should have left him to it. Why, because as I sat down and started talking to him, he went crazy, saying leave me alone. He threw a nice wee jab that I just managed to slip, but he caught me with another as I went back up. Right across the floor I went table with chairs flying everywhere. I jumped to my feet and went back at him, but we were separated before any real damage was done. It was my pride that was hurt mostly, I haven't been knocked over by a former world champion before. Any way I took stock, me from fife in a Leith

Kens dad, Tommy, passed away

Walk pub, where Ken is idolized and there were a good few people in there. So, I left him to it. I walked up the road to another pub, rattling my brains with what the fuck tae do now, no digs lol.

So, the only other person I knew was Jimmy Paste who used to share a flat with Ken, he stayed just up the road. I rang his doorbell and thank fuck he is in. I go up the stairs to his door and he said, "What the fuck happened to you?" I dint notice, but I had a wee nick on my face, so I explained what had happened. He said, "Right Jock you sit tight, I am going to find him." "Nah its fine Jimmy he is just emotionally fucked at the moment" I replied. "Aye, maybe but you're his pal, he can't do this."

So, I sit with a can of beer with another lad just talking shit, when, after about 30 minutes, in walks Jimmy with Ken. Ken says "Sorry Jock, you ken I love you and would never hurt you. "Hurt me" I said with a wee chuckle, "Yir lucky this wasn't in Methil, they would have just let us get on with it, and I would have kicked yir arse." So, it ended on a bright note. Where did I sleep? On Jimmy's couch. Hard as fuck it was and I had to keep my good suit on due to it being cold, but Jimmy if your reading this, many thanks pal, it was better than the street lol. Ken phoned me a couple of days after wards, still on the drink I'll add, and again apologised. I just said it was all fine pal, "Phone me when you come back?" "Any time."

Round 10

"Like a boxer in a title fight, you have to walk
in that ring alone." - Billy Joel

My MBE? Hahaha Me, with an MBE

It came as a great shock, but also a great honour, to receive a letter from
"the palace" to say that I have been nominated to receive an MBE, in the
New Years, Honours List (2014) for services to charity. I found out it was
Alex and Catherine from my local pub in Scone, Kinnears Inn, and a
women called Anne Marie, who in fact walked with myself and others
across the Gobi desert in Mongolia for 2 very good charities, who had
nominated me. So, it was all arranged, and I was to be presented my medal
in Scotland at Hollyrood Palace no less. I was very happy with that due
to my son Stuart saying he would bring my grandchildren along on the
day.

So, who do I take into the palace as my guest? First it had to be the
wife Christine, then, as the norm so I was informed, is to take those who
nominated you. So, Alex and Catherine were next but as invites were
limited, there was no place for Anne Marie unfortunately. Neither was
there any places left for other members of the family that I would have
liked to have had present, Janet, Jim, Willie and Arlene, sorry. Alex
booked the four of us into an apartment, not far from the palace, for the
Monday and Tuesday with Tuesday being the day of presentation. That

would be the first of July. Me and Christine got the train through and were met at Waverly station by Alex & Catherine, who drove us round to the apartment. Alex, unfortunately, put a nice dent/scrape on his car in the process of squeezing through a small gap on route. He got his ear well bashed for that lol.

Anyway, it was a beautiful apartment. Right, kilt (Scottish Highland dress) etc. hung up and now time to get some much-needed food and drink into us lol. So, onto the Royal Mile it is then where we found the nearest pub and had a bar lunch. We then phoned Ken and Carol Anne to say we had arrived into Auld Reekie, Edinburgh's unsavoury name from the 1700s, safely and where should we meet up? "How about Leith" Ken says? "Aye nae bother we will start walking down from the Princes Street end and meet you, you start making you're way up." sorted. What we never said was that we would be stopping off in every pub on the way down lol. At one stage as we cross a bridge at the top of Leith, I see a stall, which was manned by the SNP (Scottish National Party) looking for signatures regarding the Scottish Independence Referendum. This was the first time I have ever signed in support and wrote my name as an MBE holder.

When we eventually meet up, Ken and Carol Anne, I think, been doing the same as us? Not to worry they were both in good form, a great couple. But I did at some point say now folks not too much off a heavy night as I meeting the queen tomorrow? Which of course fell on deaf ears to no surprise to me. We headed back to the apartment at about 1am in the morning, but I in fact never even made my bed that night, and instead, slept on the couch lol. We had a great time in Leith with some good photos taken as well. We left Ken and Carol Anne to walk the short distance back to their flat, whilst we jumped in a taxi and headed back to the Royal Mile for last orders. So, the next day I am being woken at about 8:30 by Christine who is shouting, "Have you seen the time, it's 8:30, you meet the queen in a few hours." No long lie in then eh? Alex is up nae bother with Catherine, busy doing her nails etc. (that went on for ages lol).

The four of us looked quite fresh as we entered the Palace. The lady's had to leave their handbags at the reception area, but I got in with my Sgian-dubh, (Small Scottish knife, part of the Highland Dress), in my sock? we were then split into two groups, Alex Catherine and Christen going one way (main hall) and I was ushered into a smaller hall to wait for a briefing. There must have been 50 of us all receiving awards that day. I am thirsty and head for the drinks table, it's soft drinks all round then? Honest, I could have drunk the four large glass containers myself, boy I had a druth on me. (Thirst due to excessive alcoholic drinking.)

Finally, we got our briefing telling us that our names from this day on will be changed for ever. Then we all lined up ready to meet the Queen. I got chatting to an old lad in front of me who said he was apprehensive about meeting the Queen. "Aren't we all I said, but hey it will be fine, how about a wee dram to settle your nerves?" Aye, that would be good, if only" he said? As quick as a flash I bring out my hipper which was in the sporran, lol. "Here you go pal have a quick swig, it will do you gid." I look up only to see a camera looking straight at me. Ah fuck it, I huv done it now I thought. I had booked and paid for a video and CD of the presentation, but I don't think I'll be back for my knighthood lol

My MBE? Hahaha Me, with an MBE

I stand proud as punch in front of the head of state, a very knowledgeable lady, who was briefed on many of the charity trips I had been on. I sit at the back of the room with the other people who had been presented with their award and when the queen had left, I walked down to meet up with my guests. Were they talking about the medal? No. "Jock, did you see the queen's underclothes?" "What?" Seemingly the position the queen was standing in, on a small platform with the sun shining through the window, you could see her underskirt? "Eh no I was standing in front of her" I says lol. So, I now head off outside to meet up with son and grandchildren, at the front of the palace as the sun was splitting the trees. Hundreds of photos were taken and god did I now need a pint.

I then phoned Carol Anne to ask where they were? "We are walking just doon the mile she says." "No probs we are just walking up, see you soon." Ten minutes later there they both are, late but dressed very smart, so, next stop another bar lunch on the mile for everyone. We found a nice couple of tables outside a bar, the Burns, I think. Callum, my grandson wanted to wear my medal, so, no probs, there you go. Next Eilidh Wanted it on. As quick as a flash Ken took out his. It just so happened he had it pined into the inside of his suit jacket. Strange that eh? So, now both my grandchildren are running about the royal mile wearing our MBE medals. One day my son will sit them down and show them the photo again and explain who the other medal belonged to, a real Scottish sporting legend. After lunch we head up the Royal Mile to watch the street artists, but it was a very hot day, too hot for the grandchildren.

My son very wisely said, "I think we will head back to the station and jump on the next Glasgow train, as the bairns are far too hot." I was well made up that they all were there, on my special day. We took more photos, with everyone posing with Ken, then said our goodbyes and wished them a safe journey home to Airdrie.

We in turn hit every bar on the mile then walked our way down into the Grass Market. After about 3 or 5 bars Carol Anne said "Kens getting tired so we will head back home." "No probs again and thanks for coming." "Oh, that's ok Jock we would never have missed it for the world" Carol Anne said. Ken, well he just hugged us all then they headed for the bus, as for us well it was the Cannon Gate next. During this time, Alex had been in contact with a couple we knew from the village, who were attending the garden party that afternoon. They wanted to meet up somewhere for a pint. Spats and Val, the couple, eventually met up with us and we went into a wee bar which had live music on. Again, a good time was had by all, then it was back to the Royal Mile, and Spats and Val headed for their train home. Us? Well we kept on drinking, oh and another meal, in the Worlds End pub. What a great bar & restaurant.

The Duran road show

I received an email from Mark peters (18th September 2007) it reads:

Hi Jock, further to our telephone conversation regarding Ken Buchanan's appearance requirements during the forthcoming tour with Duran, two other promoters, (namely Keith Mayo and Wally Dixon), have both requested Kens presence at their events, therefore the dates are follows:

1. Saturday 6th October, venue Swindon, promoter Keith Mayo fee £600.

2. Tuesday 9th October Liverpool John H Stacy fee £600.

The Duran road show

3. Wednesday 10th October Manchester, Mark peters & Wally Dickson promotions, fee £600.

4. Thursday 11th October Essex Mark peters, System 1 promotions, fee £600.

5. Friday 12 October London Mark peters System 1 promotions, fee£600.

Ken will need to be available to at 6:45pm for a short brief with respective promoters and commence, meet and greet with guests at 7pm prompt. He will be paid cash. Both Mark and myself have agreed a fee of £600 per evening, with both travel and accommodation also be provided. Regarding transportation, I've spoken to Martin Devlin, (the Guy bringing Duran over). He has booked first class train tickets from Manchester to London on the morning of the 11th. My plan would be that if ken were on the same train, I could arrange a limo to collect him and Duran together. They could then be taken straight to the hotel and then onto the venue. Also, the following day, Ken could travel with Duran into London for the event on the 12th, this would make life easier I am sure? Cheers Mark.

It was a great plan lol, but it didn't work out that way? Ken did not attend the Swindon venue on day one. I phoned Ken about him not turning up at Swindon and assured him that it's not a disaster, it's only a setback, however to get back on track he must phone Mark Peters, and assure Mark that he would make the Liverpool event. (Well he didn't phone and he didn't make the Liverpool event either).

So, I get a phone call from a not to happy Mark Peters. "Jock, Ken never turned up at Swindon or Liverpool, what's happing?" "Ok" I said,

The Duran road show

"Ken hasn't been feeling to well and didn't want to tell you, he did try to make it but he was to ill. Right, how about this" I says, "Pay for me to come down with him and he will make the last three venues. I'll make sure of that, you don't even have to pay me a fee, I laughed?" (He never paid me either lol). The phone goes silent for what seemed a lifetime, then "Ok let's do it as they all want Ken to be with Duran, Jock he must get to Manchester? I will send you the tickets, get him down here?" Under my breath I am saying fuck off, and also saying yahoo, road trip lol. So, I am back on the phone to Ken. "Ken, I am coming through to get you very early Wednesday morning because we are going to Manchester" "Oh that's nice" he says, as if he didn't have a care in the world lol. Now all I have to do is break it to the Mrs? She will not be impressed but it's a road trip with legends I am thinking of, so what did I do first? I go to the pub and tell the lads, lol.

I drive through to Jimmy Pace's flat which he shares with a few other lads one being Ken. Jimmy answers the door, it's about 6am. "Fuck, hi Jock do you ken what time it is" he asks? "Aye Jimmy did Ken no tell you I was coming early?" "No, he never said a word." My next question was is he up and ready to go? "Go where" Jimmy asks?" "Manchester" I reply. Fuck no he is in his bed, he was oot last night. So, I get him up? He wants to go for a coffee, but I tell him he has no time to waste and that we will get something at the station. "Aye, where we going" he asks? "Fuck, do you no listen to a word I say, I spoke to you the other day about the Duran trip and us leaving early" I reminds him. "Sorry pal I forget." "Are you packed" I ask. "No" he says. "Right have a quick splash of water, I'll pack your case." So, I have my case and Kens as we trot up Leith walk heading to the station, there's never a taxi when you want one

173

eh and why is Ken not carrying his own case, I ask myself lol? He is still half-drunk lol lucky bugger. We just make the train and we are not long sat doon when the man with the trolley comes around. "Jock you wanting anything" Ken says. "Aye cheers I'll have a coffee and a ham roll." "Right that's a coffee and roll for my pal, and I'll have a can of beer please?" I say "If your starting this early then to hell with the coffee and roll, beer for me too please" lol. It's started, but luckily by the time we get over the border, Ken is having a wee sleep, Braw.

By the time we get to Manchester we are both looking ok, (second wind), and we go out to the taxi rank and jump into a taxi. When we say to the driver our hotel name, he says, "Are you sure you want a taxi, the hotel is not very far?" "No pal we are knackered, thanks, and no joking, he must have driven less than 200 yards. "Right lads this is it and that will be £5 he says" laughing his heed aff. Like a couple of dafties, we go on into the hotel and ask for Mark Peters room, but he is not in so we head to the bar. After about two beers, Mark Peters comes in and spots us, he is over the moon we made it and he tells us to be downstairs for 6:45pm for a small meet and greet. "Aye no probs" we say. We go to the hotel restaurant for something to eat, and of course a bottle of wine always helps.

After me ironing both our shirts and suits and cleaning my black shoes with polish (one of them spongy thing), we are almost ready to go when Ken asks me how I got my shoes looking so shinny? "I used this holding up the black boot polish sponge thing?" "Can I use it." "Aye of course, here." I go for a quick pee only to return to see Ken, with him still wearing his shoes foot flat on the floor and using the black polish sponge. I shout "stop, what are yeh doing." "Polishing my shoes" he says. "Ken lift yir foot." So,he does and sure enough there is a nice black polished shoe print on the carpet where he had went around his shoe with the sponge. He looks at me and sniggers, "I'll clean it" he says." "No you'll no" I said "you'll only make it worse. I'll have to tell downstairs (the hotel staff)." "Wait he says, what if we do this" and he covers the black footprint with the room rubbish bin. "Ooh that's ok then" I say? "A bloody bin in the middle of the room, no one will be any the wiser, leave it lets go" and we head downstairs for the meet and greet. It was a great night and at the end of the gig ken was tired and went up to his bed. It was nice to see Jimmy Batten join us on this tour as well now.

Peter asked if I would like to go with the rest of the lads to a wee club uptown in Manchester. So, Duran, me, Peter, Duran's manager, Tony Gonzales (who is also Duran's Attorney), and a couple of security lads jump into two taxis and go up town. On route I tell Peter I don't think I will have the right money for this sort of evening, but he told me it was all paid for. Braw, just what I like to hear.

So, where do we end up, only at the Spearmint Rhino club, which is a chain of strip clubs that operates venues throughout the United States, United Kingdom, and Australia. In we go, straight to the VIP suit. Wine and Champagne are the order of the night and Duran is loving it, so is the club manager because its great promotion for the club. During the evening, the strippers arrive and start chatting to us. One sits on my knee and says, "Hi do you like me?" "Aye, yir a bonny lassie" I say. "Do you want to have a dance" she asks? (Eh no thanks, that means leaving my comfy chair and drink, no danger I think to myself). "No yir ok lass I am gay" I lie. So, she moves onto Duran who is up like a flash dancing away like John Travolta, lol.

The Duran road show

We travelled to Essex by limo for the next event, but it wasn't as big a gig as Manchester, still a good laugh though and during a lunch, Ken said "I am going to punch the heed aff Duran?" Yes, he had had a few beers, but luckily me and Tony were between them both. Tony was straight up and speaking away to Duran, who thought it was all a joke, but it wasn't, Ken was blazing. It was all because Duran wouldn't give Ken a rematch after their world title bout. In fact, Ken was still haunted by the low blow thrown by Duran after the bell had rung, to end the 13th round, which would have led to a disqualification if the match had been held in the UK. In addition, Duran refused to give Ken a rematch which he richly deserved.

We soon settled both former legends back down in their seats, but that would have been a good fight, with me stuck in between them both lol. The next day, Peter, true to his word had booked first class train tickets from Manchester to London for all of us. So, Duran, Ken, me, Peter, Jimmy Batten, Tony Gonzales and couple of security lads were on our way to London. Look out London the lads are on the way lol. The train journey was a laugh, Duran is loud and very funny and when we arrive at the station, we walk outside to get into our limo, (I love saying that limo lol). We pass a stall selling coffee and snacks etc. Duran sees a tray full of doughnuts, so he just picks them up and starts handing them out to those in the group with Peter being left to pay for them all. It's now only a short drive before reaching the hotel.

Just to digress slightly, a wee story comes to mind. Ken was working as a construction tradesman in 1995 when he had a mad turn. He had found out that Duran was training in New York, so he downed tools one afternoon, boarded a plane and went in search of Duran. Ken says "I got aff the plane half pished and found myself in Harlem. I was in a bar full of Black guys. They asked me if I knew the Scottish fighter Ken Buchanan. Aye I told them, I think I ken who yer talking about. He never did find Duran, but the trip went some way to exercising his demons.

Every morning Peter sat both me and ken down and handed out £600, which ken never got a pound off, until we were back in Leith. Why would he want money when his food and drink and accommodation was all paid for and he was happy with this set up. London was a big gig with hundred's in attendance. We were getting ready in our room and I am standing at the sink having a quick shave when next thing Ken is lying naked at my feet. He was having a shower when he slipped, grabbed the shower curtain which pulled the pole out of the wall and then fell face down onto the floor. "Fuck" he says, "what happened?" "Nothing ken nothing?" lol. At least he wasn't injured and as soon as we are ready, we head downstairs for the meet and greet. At the bottom of the stairs is Peter Devlin and the Irish boxing legend Steve Collins, both talking to Jimmy Batten.

I got Steve to phone my old pal Mike Scott and to ask him if he is coming out for a drink? Mike was over the moon. Steve was a great lad. The evening was set up with a large stage in front of the audience, with a table and chair for each boxing legend to sit at. Duran then went up to the stage. The idea was that all the boxing greats would be paraded into the hall and then onto the stage, where they will be handed a mic to say how good they thought Duran was. So, the legends took it in turns to bum Duran up, all doing a great job. Ken was last to speak, and before he said his peace, he looked at me and winked. He took the mic and then stood up and sang four verses of Scotland's national anthem "Flower of

Scotland", then handed the mic back to the MC and sat back down. Honest, I could nae get off the floor for laughing lol, it was brilliant. This was a long, long night with lots of photos etc. Ken pushed me up to get my photo taken with Duran, which I did and the next day it was back on the train to Bonny Scotland.

We slept most the way back and once we got into Edinburgh, we were fresh as daisy's. A quick taxi up to Kens flat and it was then and only then I handed him £1,800 for his three days' wages. He said, "Christ I forgot about getting paid for that trip, cheers Jock, you have to take some money." "No pal it was an honour to be there." "No, you must." I said "I'll tell you what, you get the drink in all night, and we will call it quits? Jimmy paste again said I can sleep on the couch if I want to, an offer which I gladly accepted. Another excellent trip in the company of Ken again.

Back to hospital?

Ken, and his partner Carol Anne, were given an invitation to attend my nephew Sean's wedding in Kirkcaldy in fife. They were well looking forward to it, as I have previously said Kens family and ours go away back many years, so come the day, no show? So, a couple of days after the wedding I phoned Kens number, but it goes straight to his voice mail. So, I phoned Carol Anne who told me he was on the drink, ok no probs I'll catch him another day. But it wasn't to be. This went on for a full month until I got a sobbing call from Carol Anne saying, "Jock he is in hospital again?" And this time the papers got a hold off it?

The sun newspaper had a big story with photos of Ken, not good eh? Any way he was in a local Edinburgh hospital, so I went through, picked up Carol Anne, and went in to visit him. She was in bad state, shaking

Back to hospital?

like mad, I told her to get a grip, (Aye Army discipline never leaves ye), as she was the visitor not the patient. When we saw Ken, he was crying begging us to take him home just to get him out of there. He looked bad, not shaven for weeks, real skinny and so sad. We sat him down and tried to explain to him that he would be in for a good wee while and it's the best place for him. Well, he actually spent 3 months in the hospital, with only a couple of weeks freedom spent in Dundee.

He got out, but he was not 100 per cent himself. After all the treatment and the hours of talking to him it never really sunk in, and to be honest, I didn't think he knew why he was in there? He did make a trip down to London for the Henry Cooper golf weekend. He also spent a night over at mine. We had dinner and a couple of beers in Perth, accompanied by one of my old army pals and his wife, Dave and Sheena Easton. It was a nice wee chilled day, nothing daft and Ken was soon back in hospital again a month later.

I got home at 1am one morning from work to see a message on my answer Machine, "Jock, I huv had a fall and I am in hospital." So, I phoned his mobile that morning and found out he was in the Little France hospital in Edinburgh. So, I travelled over that day to find him not injured but very confused. He was found wandering the streets not knowing where he was. He thought folk or people were out to get him. The police brought him to A&E, (he was not drunk either), and he kept saying there is someone in his room. It was of course empty apart from us two. I was put down as his next of kin, as sad to say his sons and daughter never kept in touch with him. His brother, Alan is in Canada, and he had fallen out with Carol Anne, (who I think still really cared about him). He got moved back to the hospital in Morningside, Edinburgh, the one he was in before,

Back to hospital?

and at the moment, as I type, he is still there. Even the nurses remember me from my last visits?

I travelled from Scone to Edinburgh every 2nd day to take in clothes, sweets, orange juice etc. I even took his washing home to be done. He never had his reading glasses with him, so I bought him a couple of cheap pairs to tide him over. What a man. One day he started playing snooker in a games room against me and the bugger beat me, without his glasses and he's not well, lol. During this time, I had been organizing along with the very generous Bill Hopkins, a financial adviser who had his own business in the Aberdeen area, a road trip with Ken. This would see him doing some work and visiting Wick, a place he has always wanted to go to due to his dad's family coming from that area. So, with a planned 5 days on the road and everything in place, thanks to Bill and his contacts, all we need is Ken to be well enough to go on the trip. Fingers crossed because its only one month till trip starts?

Round 11

"A boxer is always armed."
- Mokokoma Mokhonoana

Plan of the Road Trip BOSS

How Bill put the road trip to me:

FRIDAY:

If I could meet you in Inverurie at 11.30am. The town is on A96 Aberdeen to Inverness Road

We are meeting Mr. Gary Cox owner of Edwards Pub and diner and Disco he will expect pictures with him and his punters. (Need to finalise small details with him). Home to mine where I become Chauffer and we see Karen. Ken to do signing off stuff if ok.

3pm Oilfast, to confirm, but I have said I would give him signed glove in return for buying tickets along with Ken getting his picture taken, standing next to a lorry and the Director. Maybe another quick photo shoot?

Home for 4 or 5pm and relax with a spot of dinner before we go to Insch Golf Club for 7pm where we have a photographer arranged and an MC to keep the night going with a raffle and quiz. We are trying to arrange a backdrop of Kens fights too.

Plan of the Road Trip BOSS

Ken to greet and open Q&A, building in with stories of Ali, Edinburgh, Watt, Duran etc. Ken will then be moved to a position where pictures with punters are taken. Our man will take email addresses to email the pictures to the punters whilst I am sure mobile phone pics will be taken. Maybe Ken going round the tables. I can introduce him to names. Does Ken do a Karaoke song? Then entertainment starts to release Ken to relax and enjoy the night. (we leave when you say).

SATURDAY:

Booked into the Royal Highland Hotel Inverness, you have a twin room B&B, Karen and I will stay there as kids come up on Sunday. Arrive around 12 o'clock, Ken pics on stair with the owner and staff, choosing light lunch and we will be off to Nairn County FC, they play Fort William with a 3pm kick off.

Meet Les Fridge then introduced to the Directors with a buffet after the game then a quiet beer and Ken hands over Man of the Match award and probs get Nairn County top. We relax for the rest of the evening. I have booked a table at the Fairways Golf Club Inverness, for a nice meal with a few quiet beers (on me). Then back to Royal Highland Hotel nightcap.

SUNDAY:

Jock, Ken, Karen and I have breakfast at a time that suits then sadly we will say goodbye for the moment as you and Ken travel to Wick.

You are both booked into the Mackays Hotel, Union Street, Wick. KW1 5ED 01955-602323 Owner Murray Lamont. I have said you will arrive, 12:30 to 1:00pm. You will be given evening meal and B and B in a Twin room in return for signing pictures with Murray and his punters.

I have a friend of a friend getting Information on Kens Mum, Catherine McManus and his dad Thomas Buchanan, which I will pass on I hope this is to you and Kens liking

From the UNDERBOSS. (Bill)

Brian, one of the senior nurses was a real help. Right down to earth sort of lad, a Dundee supporter for his sins, he was one of the nurses who helped with Ken on his last visit to the same ward months ago, when I couldn't get in to see him. I phoned every day asking how the man was and some of the nurses, who recognized my voice, would tell me the truth. Others, nah, all I got was aye he is fine, settled, sleeping just now? I didn't want that, I wanted the truth, so that when I did go in I could say, "hey, I am getting reports that you're not taking your medication", or "you been losing the heed with folk", or just "you're doing ok pal, stick with it, it's all a matter of time." Anyway a few weeks pass bye and I see Ken. He is looking great, what a change, well not 100 per cent but certainly ok, much, much better. We have at least got a fighting chance with this trip. I arrange to go back in to see him again tomorrow.

Nurse Brian said we could possibly go for a coffee together with Ken at the hospital café, with a wee stretch of the legs. Well it was organised as Brian had said. Out for a coffee, not alone mind you, no, because the café was closed, we had to go out to the shop and therefore we had to have one of the other staff come along to chum us. He was not a bad lad, John was his name. Anyway, we got oor coffee and wee biscuit, and sat in the sun for a good wee while and sorted the world to rights. We spoke about everything, what Ken is going to do when he gets out of hospital, a wee holiday was spoke about, in fact it was quite emotional on Kens part. He spoke about his lassie and sons not wanting to know him, missing his dad, thanking me for being here for him. Mind you that never needed to be said, I would of in fact walked to Edinburgh if I had too, to see that he was ok.

After our chat it was back in time for dinner, for him no me, I had to get my arse back to Perth before the traffic started again. I was due into work tomorrow but will phone the hospital to ask how he is getting on as normal. Well that's me on my four days off again, so back into see the man. He was lying on his bed reading a sports book. "Oh hi pal, how are you" he asks." "Great, don't you want to go out for coffee?" "Aye fine." So, on with his trainers and jacket, well it is Scotland and its Bloody freezing. I speak to one of the nurses about us going out, "Aye nae bother, enjoy" she says, as she shows us out the ward. (what no warden, or side kick?)

We are oot on our own tae lol, none of the two hospital cafes were open, so I suggest we have a wee walk round to the shops in Morningside. We were speaking about razor blades of all things? "So Ken, you think you need more" I say, "aye, let's have a wee look in the local chemist?" So in we go. I can't see Kens blades, the normal ones he buys, but do see a bag of 8 good ones and takes them to the checkout. Ken attempts to give me money to pay for them, (£1:50 is not going to cut it I, am thinking). "Nah yir fine Ken, I'll get these you get the coffee." "Aye ok." So out the shop and straight into a wee coffee shop, two doors down where Ken finds us a table? So, I'll be ordering and paying I am thinking then, lol. We sit and blether about fitbaw and after about 30 minutes we wander back to the ward. We are in the door no more than two minutes when one of the nurses says, "Ken you have a visitor."

We turn around to see Allan Kens brother, step into the lobby, shock? They both give each other a big cuddle. Ken has a tear in his eye as we all walk into Kens room. They are both talking away. Ken asks where he is staying? In your flat he says? (My question is how did he get in there, or even better still, how did he know where Ken was, and where his flat and keys were?) Carol Anne springs to mind. Ken by the looks of his face is not too happy about this arrangement. However, it's time for me to leave and I say my goodbyes, telling Ken I'll be back on Wednesday. I shake Allan's hand and give Ken a cuddle, well that was a turn up for the books, was it no?

Anyway, Allan is up for the week, so Carol Anne says. "He is staying at Kens flat and having tea with me" she told me. Then Ken gets news he is to move hospitals, for the better. It was on the cards anyway and he is now on the Oxgangs road area. I spoke to one of the senior nurses to ask how he is settling in and she replied, "Oh he is fine, he is handing out sweeties as we speak to the other folk in the hospital." I spoke to her about our plans to go north, etc. She said the senior nurse and consultants were going to have a meeting regarding Ken and would get back to me, if permission was granted for this trip.

Guess what it wasn't? Yep its off. All that planning, by both myself and Bill was in vain. The doctors said if he went, he would not get back into hospital to carry on with his treatment. So, I said if that's the way it is, that's that, Kens health comes first. I spoke to Bill regarding what was said, and he was fully supportive of the decision, so I took the decision to

Plan of the Road Trip BOSS

do the trip myself. I must be aff ma fucking heed, I said to myself. I visited Ken for the last time before my trip north. He signed a few items which I was going to give to Bill to hand over to his two charity's which he supports. Here is a rough detail of my couple of days/ nights and the weather was great.

7th October

Flower shop for 10am (flowers for Bills wife and lady from the registrar office in wick)

Depart (Home) 12 midday

Arrive at Insch Train Station, next to Gordon terrace, along south road say 4pm,

3 hours journey, Via Ballater, about 100 miles approximately and stay at Bills overnight.

8th October

Depart Clatt (bills) at approximately 10am. A9 and A96, (Elgin, Inverness) 4 hours 30 mins 176 miles.

Arrive at wick approximately 3pm, stay about 2 hours? Wick Highland council Office on the 8th of October Girnigoe Street Wick. KW1 4HW, the registrar Elaine Gray office number if needed 01955-609523--She is getting archived pictures of the very house Ken was brought up in and his family tree history.

Depart wick at 5pm. arrive home at 12pm (5hr drive) 205.97 miles approximately depending on traffic and weather possibly stay in inverness in B&B that evening? Home Friday morning.

Plan of the Road Trip BOSS

I Must say the plan went like a dream, Bill and his wife Karen could not have done enough for me. Every detail, food, drink, bed etc. was 100 per cent. I was well looked after, and their two lads were great fun. Next morning, as I was heading off to Wick, Karen made me a great wee peace (Scottish sandwiches) so there was no need to stop on the way up. A big thanks for that.

So, I was 10 minutes from wick when I called the registrar's office to say I will soon be arriving for my meeting with Elaine Grey, who had kindly put together Kens dad's family tree. "Oh I am sorry Mr. Mcinnes, but she is not in the office this morning due to her having to work in the Thurso office, as someone had phoned in sick, but all the paperwork is waiting for you here in wick." No problem I said to myself over 300 miles of travel and I can't speak to the person as per my plan, but the ladies in the office were very nice and again could not do enough for me, (they must have guessed I was a fifer lol). So, once the photos had been taken it was down the road back home, but I had to stop off in Aviemore at a B&B due to being shattered, plus Scotland were playing on the telly lol and I cannie miss that one.

Well the following week, on my days off, I popped into the centre to see the man, and show him what was given to me up in Wick and of course show him the photos of my trip north, lol. And, never forgetting the hospitality of both Karen and Bill who looked after me like a king the night before I went onto the 2nd half of my trip. To say Ken was over the moon was an understatement. He was proud as hell, reading all about his family from his father's side, aye a wee tear in the big lad's eye for sure. The following week, I phoned the centre again to arrange another wee visit and a nurse put me straight through to Ken. "Oh, hi Jock how are you." "Aye fine, I was looking to pop in and see you on Sunday or Monday?" "Aye no bother but?" Big pause. "What's the problem" I said. "Oh, it's just that I am going home back to the flat on Tuesday about 4pm and don't have a lift?" Straight out of the blue that one, not sure if it's a step in the right direction or not but hey he has been in one hospital or another for months, so I said I will pick him up. "Oh, that's great pal, see you then." I asked to speak to the senior nurse in charge and asked her about Ken leaving. She said they have seen a massive difference in him over the last we while and it was his decision, he will be missed? He is a great laugh and spends time speaking to the others about his career etc. I had mixed emotions, I would have preferred him to go the full distance with his treatment and on the other hand he sounded so happy.

So, its Tuesday and I walk up to the hospital front door, which is glass, and who do I see staring back at me? Yip Ken, standing waiting on me. He gave me a big cuddle and said, "Are you ready?" "Me, aye, are you." "Oh aye, I had the bag backed since early morning." He got a wee talking too from the senior nurse regarding taken his medication at the right time etc. and that they love him to bits, but don't want to ever see him back again. Ken went round everyone to say his goodbyes and they even had a nice wee card for him, aye a wee tear again.

He kept his biggest cuddles for all the nurses, which he had told me a hundred times do a great job. I had to take a minute out to sign a wee document saying he is ok with the moving out and how I thought he was treated whilst staying at the centre. (I was of course his nominated next of kin).

We load up the car, Ken waves goodbye, and we are off heading to Leith and his wee flat. It's typical teatime traffic in the capital, bloody crazy lol. Ken talks like there is no tomorrow all the way back, finishing off by saying he will never drink again, well no like that any way. Its Pishing it doon as we get into the flat. He picks up the mail and looks around. The flat look's neat and tidy, someone has been in. The TV works and he has heating but no food, 2 out of 3 is no bad said Meat Loaf. So, he puts his coat on and walks me back to my car, says goodbye in the normal way rain or no rain, big cuddle and waits till I am on the right road north. He looks so happy. I phoned him the next day to find him at the gym speaking to the lads.

After a wee while I phoned Ken up. "How are you pal?" "Aye ok pal and you?" "Good, working away, what you up to." "Not a lot but don't know if ah telt ye but Edinburgh council are looking to do a wee thing with me, a kind of reception with me winning the world title many years ago." "Eh not sure if you did." So, he said "Give me your address, (like I haven't done that a thousand times before) and I'll get an invite oot to you?" "Cheers pal, that will be nice." So, he got it again. Three days later, I give him another phone call, no answer, nae problem, I will phone again and after about two weeks of trying I have still not got hold of him? Sounds like trouble, yip, sure enough when I do effectually catch up with him, he is back on the drink but sounding ok. We have words? But as he says, "Jock what have I got left?"

Fuck he sounds so sad. I arrange to meet up with him before Christmas for dinner in Edinburgh. So, it's all arranged, he will meet me and a good former black watch man, Davy Bryce, at Waverley station about 11:30ish. So, on the day, Davy gets on at his stop at Kirkcaldy in good spirits, even better after I hand him a can of beer. I try to phone Ken but no answer. We get into Edinburgh, get off the train and head to the bar. Davey stands

Dundee charity day and night

in the que whilst I try to get a hold of Ken and after 5 minutes he answers. "Where the hell are ye Ken, you were meant to meet us at the station?" "Sorry Jock, I slept in." "Ok pal no probs we will jump in a taxi and head down to you in Leith, where do you want to meet up." "The Central he says." "Yip no problem ah ken it well? So, we head for a taxi.

We blether all the way down to Leith and we get dropped off at The Central bar. There's the man. He greets me like he hasn't seen me in years, and he is dressed smart as fuck as normal. I introduce him to Davy, and they get on like a house on fire. "So, what's the plan Ken?" "Not sure, whatever you want?" "How about lunch for starters?" "Aye great let's go to my pal's boozer up the road." So, after a wee while and a couple of photos taken by a passer bye, we are in another pub. We chat, whilst taking in the menu, it's normal pub grub but it looks great. I leave Ken and Davy to blether whilst I go to the toilet and pay the bill. Yip, I don't even have the grub and its paid for, who said I was tight lol.

To cut a long story short after the meal we do another couple of bars, then back to The Central, where a few photos were taken, an honest, short but great day. Ken was looking good, although on the drink, but as he says what else does he have to do? Davy was loving it, I think this made his week, month year etc. So, time is marching on as they say, we said our goodbyes and jumped into a taxi leaving Ken sitting with a couple of pals, so that was another day out with the legend.

Dundee charity day and night

I was asked by doctor death, real name John smith (CSM, Company Sergeant Major), if I could do him a favour and get Kens autograph. It's for one of his pal's grandsons, who was doing a project at school on Scottish sporting legends. "Yeh, I am pretty sure that can be arranged."

So, the following week I met up with Ken and he signed a pair of gloves and a photo for me. So, I emailed John and said I had a signed photo for the young lad. "That's great" he replies, telling me that he is up in Dundee in a couple of weeks for a regimental dinner. (see I never get invites to these?)

So, to get back to my story, I meet up with John along with a couple of old pals. He is over the moon. "Fantastic Jock" he says, "you did very well, I'll not forget this." Sure enough, a wee while after, I get a message. "Jock, the Dundee branch of the black watch association want to run a charity evening for your next challenge, Nepal." Fantastic, that's great I thought. He said he had invited along the Fife, Perth and Angus branches as well, as its going to be a games day challenge, darts, pool, etc. There will also be a raffle and auction. "Oh great, sounds like fun" I said, oh and it was, due to the competition starting early, on the Saturday afternoon in Dundee.

I asked Ken if he was alright for me picking him up on the Friday before. "Aye no bother" was the reply. So, I picked him up as planned and we sat in with couple of beers that night. Then, next morning we got up nice and early as my pirate pal, Gordon Cruikshank's (former RSM, Regimental Sergeant Major) in my old regiment, had invited us both to his house, only 2 doors down, for breakfast. Dennis, the pub landlord, was also invited. So, we knocked on his door and sat down along with Gordon, his son, Andrew, and Dennis to a spread that would have fed a platoon. Honest, he did us all proud. At one point during breakfast, Andrew said to his dad (Gordon), dad, these sausages are harder than Ken, referring to his cooking of course lol. Next it was back to the house for a quick spray of aftershave and out the door into a taxi, which would take us all into

Perth to meet up with the minibus. This would take us to the Black Watch club in Dundee, a trip off about 30 minutes.

So, we all trooped in, met up with John Smith, Colin Gray, and Dave Young the organizers of the competition. We had to get ourselves into teams of 6, so it was me, Ken, Winky Greer, and 3 other lads. (sorry forgot their names). Gordon, Andrew and his son were in another team again, but I can't mind who else, but it will come back to me one day? (We actually won the pool part of the competition).

My brother Willie and his partner were also in attendance. It's always great to meet up with him as he is a great laugh. So, it was game on, where each team played every other team, with the end score going on a big board. We played darts, pool and a few other pub games. During the day, an old pal of both mine and my brothers turned up, Freddie Forbes, a die-hard Dundee FC supporter and a very good lad. Talking about Dundee FC, another very good friend of mine, Steve Martin, who was the director at Dundee fc, has done me proud on a few occasions. Firstly, by having both me and Ken attend (hospitality) a game at Dens Park, and then presenting in front of the supporters at a full house. Ken kindly returned the favour by signing a few boxing gloves for Steve.

Me and Steve also organised a charity trek to Morocco once, for the club, and it was a great laugh. It was a first for any such team in Scotland. Anyway, back to Freddie. He presented me with a beautiful montage of cards and photos of every football strip my team, East fife fc, has ever worn which was in a massive frame. In my head I am thinking, how am I getting this home, I am going to well pished after this gig. We also had a raffle and an auction, for which I had brought along some really good items. Some never got sold, but I left them for any future events the Dundee club might hold.

At the end of the games day Ken, was asked to go up on stage with JJ Smith and Colin Gray, who as I said organised the day's events. They thanked everyone for attending and of course for Ken supporting the day and presented me with a cheese. Also, in attendance was Ronnie Proctor who said his association will also support me with a donation, Fife and Perth branches said they will also do the same. They reneged on that but that's another story.

British Ex-boxer's hall of fame

I Received a nice phone call from my welsh Bro, Phil Jones, saying, Ken has been nominated as an inductee into the British ex-boxer's hall of fame, and would I accompany him down to Hastings. The only problem with this was Ken was in lockdown in hospital, where I had been visiting him on my days off for at least two months. He was suffering Alcohol Related Brain Damage, and he was back at Penumbra Milestone alcohol free care home, at Milestone house, 113 Oxgangs Road North, Edinburgh. Yip, Ken has Alcohol Related Brain Damage (ARBD). So what is this ARBD? It is the term that is used to describe a range of symptoms such as, memory loss, loss of concentration, feeling confused, irritated, or having difficulty making choices and decisions. It is important to remember that with the right care support and treatment, people with ARBD can make a significant recovery. Penumbra Milestone is a step-down unit for people with ARBD, who no longer require medical intervention, yet they are currently in an acute hospital setting and cannot go directly home without support.

British Ex-boxer's hall of fame

Through the provision of intensive, multidisciplinary support and treatment the unit will, improve outcomes for people with ARBD who are in acute hospital in Lothian, and reduce the number of days that people with ARBD spend in acute hospital settings, despite no longer requiring acute medical care. The unit will provide re-enablement support to people for up to 12 weeks. Penumbra, a third sector organization will manage the 10 bedded unit, there will also be NHS staff providing in-reach support (physical, psychiatrist, psychologist, occupational therapist, physiotherapist and community substance misuse nurses.) There is also social work support available.

So, I said to Phil I will pop through ASAP and speak to the medical staff and Ken regarding this. So they agreed, but they said I would have to ensure he did not drink and he must take his medication every day, and of course you Mr. Mcinnes will have to sign to say you will do this, and ensure he returns straight back here afterwards? Yes, I will do whatever you say, but in my head, I am saying how the hell am I going to do all that? I phoned Phil to say Ken and me will be down and asked what the arrangements were.

Before we go down South, I am thinking Ken needs a new suit. I have a good friend who used to work in kilt shop in Perth, but now works in Slater's Dundee, Michelle, who was once married to a black watch lad. So, I give her a call. "Can you fit Ken for a suit on the house" I ask. She knows about Ken with me regularly going into the kilt shop for a blether. "I'll ensure you and the shop receive a signed personalized photo, framed etc." "No problem Jock we can do this." So, the week before we have to fly down South, I drive from Perth to Leith, pick up Ken, and drive to Dundee to meet Michelle and the manager of the shop. We get photos taken then Ken gets a new suit, shirt, tie, even socks and a hanky. Well done Michelle, brilliant work. Kens over the moon as I drive him back to Edinburgh then me back to Perth. That was a few miles driving, but hey, Ken will look smart as fuck down at the awards day.

So, the instructions were, fly from Edinburgh to London where you will meet up with Dick McTaggart and his good lady, who will be flying down from Glasgow. Dave Harris, the organizer, will meet you in London, and drive you all down to hasting's by Mini bus, about 1 hour's drive (which in fact took 2 hours due to traffic, but hey look at the company I, am in).

We meet Phil, who is waiting for us at the hotel where we book in. We sort out our room, with three of us sharing the one room, braw. It's now time for breakfast/brunch. Staying at the hotel unknown to us were all the ex-professional boxers, strange that eh, but they are a great bunch of lads. After breakfast me Phil and Ken go for a wee walk around Hastings. It's a nice day with braw weather and we had a coffee in a wee cafe, then onto the pier where we took some photos.

In the evening we had a meal in the hotel, then sat with the welsh lads and spoke about boxing. Ken said he is going to his bed, yet it must have been only about 8pm. He never touched one drink all night, good man. Phil and me took turns at just popping in to the room to check on him, sound asleep, and us, well we stayed for a good wee drink with our welsh brothers. Next day we had breakfast, then had a wee walk before getting the transport to the venue, which was down by the sea. It was a really smart location and while we were waiting to get in, due to the large crowd, we spoke with Alan Minter and a couple of other lads. When we eventually got in, we found our table was a good bit away from the main stage, but it was next to a door we could open due to the heat. Yes, it was a roasting day. So, the five of us, counting Dick and his good lady took our seats. Joining us at the table was Frank Bruno, John Conteh, and a couple of older retired referees.

The day progressed, the meal was great as was the drink and Ken never touched a drop. That made my job easy. As more and more people were going up for their awards, I said to Dick, "any idea when you will be up?" "Nah" he says, then out of the blue, there is an announcement on the mic, will Mr. Jock Mcinnes please come up to the stage. Dick says to me, "Jock you're on?" I am laughing, surely it cannie be me? But, "Yep" Phil says, "It was your name pal." So, I go up and speak with Dave Harris the main man. "Jock someone hasn't turned up, so would you present the award to Dick for us?" Would I? Yir fucking dam right, I think to myself. "Off course" I reply. "Thanks," he says.

As I turn to sit down, he grabs me. "Where are you going" he says? "Waiting for you to call us both up" says the bold me? "Nah, you have to do the small introduction and call up Dick yourself." With 600 folk, all staring at me, right, off the cuff it is then, lol. I speak for a couple of minutes but I can't remember what I said, however, they must have liked it as they all laughed. So, I call up Dick, present him with his award and we both sit down. I haven't felt so proud since my Son's wedding, honest, for a good fifer like me presenting such an award to a fellow scot, a Dundee man, made me burst with pride. Next it was Phil's turn as he presented Ken with his award. We were like two School Boys who just found a porn book lol. Many, many photos were taken but hours' later I was still so happy I could have bought a round. Fortunately, Phil had that covered lol.

British Ex-boxer's hall of fame

After many hours of being in the company of Britain's greatest collection of boxers, it was time to head back to the hotel. What's next? Yep, you guessed it, in the bar till the small hours. Ken went to his bed early again as he was tired and again, me and Phil took turns to see that he was ok. In the morning we pack up and it's a reverse of our journey down here to get home. Not before taking many photos with Phil and the ex welsh boxers though, great lads. My car was parked at Edinburgh airport, so it was a short drive back to the hospital for Ken, who looked tired but happy, then me, well I drove back to Perth happy as fuck. What an honour for a wee man from Methil, I'll remember that day for many years to come.

Round 12

"I don't hit bad people, I just give them a shape, like
Blacksmith shapes a iron!"- Mikki Koomar

Welsh Boxing Award Ceremony

My welsh brother phones me. "Jock how would you like to attend along
with Ken, the welsh ex Boxers awards?" "Yeh, sounds good to me."
When he gives me the date and timings, I realise that I will have to drive
down to wales. Seemingly Ken is aware as Phil phoned him but just in
case, I give him a call. "Hi Ken, you ok for this welsh trip next month?"
"What welsh trip?" "It should be in your diary, have a wee check." "Right
give me a minute." From the background noise he is in a pub. "Ken, are
you in The Central?" "Aye, oh aye got something about it here?" "Good
man, look, I'll phone you a couple of days before we depart to give you a
time when I will be through to pick you up." "Right that's great, what are
we doing again? So, I go through it all again with him.

So, with a few days to go I phone The Central bar. Gill one of the great
staff members that keep a wee eye out for Ken answers, (his phone was
off). "Gill is Ken in?" "Yeh, hold on honey here he is." "Hi Ken, it's
me." "Oh, hi Jock I, am in The Central." "Ah Know, I phoned it. Right,
I'll be at yours very early Thursday morning, about 4am." "Right that's
ok, I'll be ready." "Ok, how will I get into the flat as the flat door will be

locked?" "Buzz me on the intercom and I'll let you in. If not just phone my mobile." "Ok, that's great see you then, enjoy your pint.

Lynnette, Gordons wife, gave me a sat nav so I could put the post code in that Phil had given me and hopefully not get lost in Wales. I would have been fucked otherwise, yes, I can read a map, but can't do both i.e. read a map and drive. So, I leave Perth at about 3am as I hate being late and arrive safely at Kens. I phone his mobile, no joy, I buzz his flat again no joy. Fuck, I try his mobile about 8-10 times, nothing. So, I press a service button on the wall pad. Someone answers, a lady. I explain I'm trying to get hold of Ken. Somehow, she gets him on the phone. "Ken, I am downstairs, let me in." "Oh, ok pal, nae problem." It's now 4:30am, Ken is ready, standing in his suit with bag in hand. "Ken, we are going to be sitting in the car for hours, you'll no need a suit on." "Nah I'll be fine" he says. Ok, so we head off and to be honest it was a journey and a half, but a good laugh was had on the way. We stopped off for breakfast just the other side of the border and sat out in the fresh air with our bacon rolls and coffee, then it starts.

"Where are we going, what is this for" asks Ken? I explain again about the Wales award night etc. Honest, if I heard this once on the eight hour journey, I heard it 50 times, poor bugger. At one point he says to me, "Jock, what's that doon there?" He is pointing into the foot well beside him. "I don't know, maybe you have dropped something. It will be ok." "Naw, there is two of them." Driving carefully and slowly, I look over. "I can't see anything." Then it hits me, Ken that's your feet." "Oh, so it is" as he chuckles to himself. Every now and again Kens phone goes, its Phil. "Hi lads, how are you getting on." Ken says "great, everything is ok we are at eh, Jock where are we?" "Sat nav says 4 hours to the post code you had given us, traffic is a nightmare" I reply.

After a lot of stopping, diversions and asking for directions from welsh folk, we say fuck it lets stop at next pub and have a wee break. "Aye, that would be nice" says the bold Ken. We are only about 5 miles from where we were to meet Phil anyway. Ken heads for the toilets and I order the drink and yes, I am on coke. The older lad behind the bar says, in a broad Welsh accent, "excuse me fella, but your friend looks like the boxer Ken Buchanan from Edinburgh." I said, "your right", and explained why we were down in wales. He is immediately on his mobile to others and when Ken gets back, the pub has a few extras in it lol. They ask for photos etc. and Ken says, "Nay bother." I take Kens mobile and phone Phil, explaining where we are etc. "Stay where you are, I'll come and get you?" lol, he is a good man is oor Phil. 10 minutes later we meet the man himself and he is in his normal good form. "Right finish your drink and follow me." Ken says, "What about me?" "You're coming too pal. We say our goodbyes and we drive for about 10 minutes, park up and arrive at a wee flat in a town just outside Merthyr. Phil says it's his pals flat, so all is good.

We make ourselves at home. It's a nice wee flat, but shame I have to share a bed with Ken, but all is good. We go out and meet up with Phil and have lunch and a couple of beers. That night Ken decides to get up and go for a pee, no problem, just climb all over the top of me Ken rather than get out of bed a walk round eh. This happened not just once but a few times. I even catch him trying to walk out the door, which I had locked thank fuck. The next day Phil picks us up to go to the venue which is not far from Cardiff. We are all suited and booted and it's a braw day.

Civic reception Edinburgh (Why?)

The award ceremony is being held in a long hall which I think is an old miners club. Anyway, we find some seats as Phil goes to the bar. It's very informal and a few of the Welsh lads come up and say hi. Cyril Thomas, who we met at British boxing hall of fame spoke to us both. We also had a quick word with Alan Minter, who was also in attendance with his good lady. Bunny Johnston was there sitting just in front of us and we sit down and enjoy our pints, but not for long. Bunny gets up and knocks the table, the drinks go up in the air, then lands all over me and Ken. Fuck, I was not impressed as I am soaked but Ken is not too bad. Bunny looks over, sheepishly, then moves down the table a bit. Phil says, "You ok there boyo?" "No am no, he's just knocked the drinks all over us. He hasn't even apologized then walks away, not even offering to buy us a drink." I am now blazing, "I am going to speak to him." "No, hold on Jock, I'll get you drinks" says Phil.

It all cools down but later I do have a word with Bunny. "Oh, am sorry pal, I never meant it" he says. Alan asked us to sit by him and we do. So after a poor start the day got better and better. Phil and the welsh lads know how to enjoy themselves and before we leave, we have photos taking outside. We don't stay out too late due to me driving the next morning. We blether shit all the way back to Scotland and we get back into Leith for about 4pm. So, it's drop the bags and round the corner for a beer, well for Ken that is, I still have an hour's drive ahead of me, the joys. But I wouldn't change these sorts of trips for the world.

Civic reception Edinburgh (Why?)

"Hi Jock, what are you doing on Friday 22nd January 2016?" "Not sure, why." "Well, the Edinburgh council Lord Provost wants to put on a civic reception for me?" "Aye that's nice but why? And its took them

Civic reception Edinburgh (Why?)

long enough has it not?" "So, you want to go then?" "Aye, it's a night out I suppose. I am working the next day so I will not stay over, and I will stay off the drink" I said. The plan was to head to Carol Anne's flat, then taxi out to the town hall for the reception. So, I arrive at Carol Anne's and Kens not there. He is at a hotel in the centre with Phil, (great lad from wales). Carol Anne introduces me to another lady, her pal, who is also going. After a short while a taxi arrives to take us up town. There was about 50+ people all dressed up for the night and free drinks were the order of the night, but not for me I am driving. I chat with Phil from wales, great lad (sure I said that before?).

I had brought with me a miniature MBE which I pinned to Kens lapel. He looked smart as fuck. Wee Willie Henderson was in attendance. He has always been a great supporter of Kens. Me, Willie and about 12 others did the Gobi Desert walk together and we played in the same football team in the Mongolian national stadium, a first for any team from the UK, but that's another story. In fact, it should be a book on its own lol, as he loves the boxing. A couple of people made some nice speeches about Ken and his career and Phil went up and gave a great speech, about his long-time friend. Well done Phil, you did yourself and your country, Wales, very proud. We stayed for about 2 hours then we tried for about 30 minutes to get Ken away from all the people wanting his signature and photo etc. He was very much in demand, but we had been invited to a club up town by a casino owner, and the transport was waiting for us. It was Kens night, so we never made a big noise about it.

We arrive at the casino and are taken through the club into a very nice private suite. It was very posh I must say, and we all take a free drink. I am driving so it's a soft drink, bugger, all this free drink and I am driving again. Sods law eh? Ken is not drinking either and everyone sits down and blethers about nothing in particular. Eats were handed out, but most of us were asking why the civic reception was given to Ken? He got nothing out of it. No freedom of the city, no declaration that there will be a statue erected in his honour. No presentation of a trophy, scroll etc., Nothing? Some nice speeches etc. but that is it. People started to head off. Wee Willie had to catch a train I think, and Ken and Phil went to a hotel. I thought the plan was for me to possibly stay at his/ Carol Anne's flat that night. I could then have a wee drink. But no chance now eh. So much for a plan. So, me, Carol Ann and her friend head back to her flat, where I said my goodbyes and drive up the road. The time was about 2am so, I will not be home until about 3am and I will be sober. Bugger lol.

Kelty Q&A

Whilst serving in the Watch, I knew a lad called Spunky Graham, real name Duncan, any way he is a Lodge man from Kelty in Fife. I asked him about the possibility of Ken and me putting on a wee Q&A evening with his member's? He said he will speak to them at the next meeting and lo and behold, long story short, he said yes. We sorted out a date and fee etc. That's great, now all I have to do is ask Ken? Yes, I didn't tell him about it due to his memory not being too sharp, (I personally think he has a touch of dementia?)

But he was good with all the arrangements, so the morning of the gig I drove to pick up Ken in Leith. I went to his flat at the time I had arranged with him, 11 to 11:30am, if I leave it to late, he hits Leith pubs, but he is not in? Ok, no problem, I'll try his local. No not there either? Bugger, but sure enough he is in the next pub having his wee half and half of larger When he sees me, it's all, "Hi Jock how are you? What are you doing down this way?" I take him for breakfast at the Foot of the Walk, a local Wetherspoons. Over breakfast I explained it all again. "Aye that's sounds good, when is this happing again he says?" Oh dear, poor bugger I thought. "Let's go and put on your other suit and fresh shirt and grab an overnight bag." "Aye lets he says." So, after this, we drive to see Billy Hanafin, a good lad from the BW who was the manager of the ice-skating rink in Kirkcaldy. This is a delaying tactic to keep Ken out the pubs and after 30minutes of talking, coffee etc. we say our goodbyes.

Billy was sharp as a button and knew the score, showing us around etc., i.e. wasting time lol. Next is a wee drive up to my Nephews house in Kennoway to see Sean, Amber and wee Jock (Lloyd). As we pull up, my sister comes to the door. "Hi Janet, how's you?" "Great, come along in and have a sit doon. I explained what we are through for, i.e. Kelty Lodge, as she makes soup for us both. Time is now marching on and after more time wasted looking at Sean's man cave, which he is in the process of building along with my brother-in-law Jim, we said our goodbyes and take a slow drive to Kelty lodge. We arrive and go straight in to meet Duncan and another old BW pal, Pat Mcalinden, who was also booked to talk that evening, about his x amount of years in the battalion. Other members arrive, then it's a sit down at the top table after introductions. Duncan had a film/video set up showing some of Kens bouts. I was impressed, then it's down to Ken.

Hands go up with member's asking questions about Kens fantastic boxing career. Unknown to Ken I had planted pre-arranged questions amongst the members, just in case things dried up. But it wasn't necessary. The evening is going well with Ken on good form. During the short interval Ken is signing things, and getting his photo taking. He is on

Shandies and I am on Irn Bru. Next, it's a raffle and auction, then it's back to the bar to end a very good night. We say our goodbyes and head back to Scone, which takes me about 30minutes as I am trying to make last orders at my local. I haven't had a drink all day.

Ken enjoyed his wee night and tried to shove money in my pocket as I drove. "What are yeh doing?" "I am no wanting it, it's yours, you worked for it." This goes on for about 10 minutes. "Ok I'll let you get the drinks in when we hit Scone?" That seems to satisfy him. We park up and go in. The pubs jumping. "What you wanting says the bold me?" "A wee bottle Jock (Budweiser)." Wait a minute what am I doing "It's your round Ken?" "Oh, ok no probs he says." Just at that moment, Tich, one of the younger lads says, No yir no buying a pint, let me get it?" "Jock you can get the next one" he says lol. 5 drinks later we walk up through the park, along with Tich, on our way home. Another good night under the belt.

Round 13

"Mental health has got to be the biggest battle I've ever fought, more so than any opponent."- Tyson Fury

Edinburgh award with my son Stuart

A newspaper article says "Ken Buchanan will be presented with the "Edinburgh Award" more than half a century on from his professional debut. The 71-year-old former lightweight champion's handprints will be immortalized in a flagstone outside the City Chambers along with those of the previous Edinburgh Award winners." Bit slow in coming I think but better late than never. Ken says he will ensure I get an invitation sent to the house and sure enough two days later I have my invitation. So, what next? I phone my son. "Hi son, want to go to a good gig with yir dad?" "Yeh, sounds good what's the plan? I explain about the whole Edinburgh award etc., "Yeh that will be great." I'll get the train though so I can have a we drink." "Great son, we will speak over the next couple of days." I am on the phone to Ken explaining my son will be in attendance and he says great no probs. On the day of the event I turn up at Kens suited and booted and park the car up as I am staying at Kens that night. He will be staying at a hotel in the town with Phil and he will meet up with me later he says,

We arrange to meet up at a wee pub two doors down from civic buildings, but before this I head into the town to meet my son coming of train. We meet up and head for a bar where I explain what the drill will be for the night. "Right Stuart, we can have a few beers before meeting up with Ken, Phil and a few of the lads at a wee pub. Then we head into the presentation all together. There is a wee reception where Ken will get his award, etc. followed by a couple of speeches, then a meal with the provost. I would like you to attend this as it's a great meal and a great evening." What I am doing is selling it to him, as past dinners of these sorts go on a bit which keeps me away from the bar lol. good luck son. Then it's into a taxi to the Casino, which is laying on a free bar, food etc.

"That sounds great dad" says Stuart. I love having a pint with my son as it's just like having a beer with my pals. He enjoys a laugh and a beer but as is the way with youngsters, he thinks he is more sensible than me when I was his age, lol. We bounce in and out of a few bars in the capital, just talking shit and having a good laugh. Then it's time to meet up with Ken, Phil and a few of the lads in another a wee bar. They are all in good form and I introduce Stuart to the lads who have already got the beers in. We take a few photos then head two doors up to the civic building's where Ken meets the press and the provost of Edinburgh. They get their photos taken, crouched down at kens handprint, which is laid out in the main entrance, along with other celebrity's.

I did notice that they hadn't even put in Kens MBE? Was that by mistake or design? After the photo shoot, we head upstairs to the reception held in a large room, which is packed with bodies. We start to break off into wee groups, and me, Phil and Stuart get ourselves a wee drink at the free bar, (love it). Ken is getting his photo taken by so many folk and wee Willie Henderson (former Rangers FC legend), a big Buchanan fan, is also in attendance. After a while the reception kicks off with the provost saying his bit, then it's a famous lady poet reciting her poem about ken and what he has achieved though out his boxing career. (I did ask her during the evening if she could possibly send me a copy, but I am still waiting?)

Ken is given a smart trophy which is the Edinburgh Award and we all get our photos taken alongside it. After a good wee while someone from the chambers announces dinner will soon be served. So, I says, "Right Stuart, you go through for dinner as we only have the one invitation." "No probs dad" he replies and as he heads off. I head back to the bar with a couple of the lads. Ken is away through as well, and in the end, the dinner went on for ages. Stuart had to leave in time to get the last train, but not before saying thanks to both me and Ken for a great night. He said he can't go back to the casino with us or miss his last train, because he was working the next day, I think. A number of taxis turn up and we all head into Edinburgh for the casino, where food and drinks were all laid on. I am sure I drunk myself sober twice lol, and after a good wee while I said to Phil "I am going back to Kens and bed pal, I am fucked." "Aye boyo, you don't look to sharp." lol (That was an understatement).

I still have no idea how I found Leith, never mind Kens flat and the next day I headed home (in the afternoon). Ken still wasn't back at the flat so he must have enjoyed his night lol, after all it was another good evening.

Another Welsh Trip 7th November 19

I pick Ken up at 9am (one and half hours before departure). Approximate travel to Edinburgh airport is 30 minutes, but we will allow an 1hr in case the traffic is heavy, to the airport. The plan is we travel on 7th November flying Edinburgh to Cardiff departing 11:30am, arriving at

Cardiff 12:55pm. We return on 9th November flying Cardiff to Edinburgh, departing at 13:55pm arriving Edinburgh 15:20pm. The accommodation will be at the Castle Hotel Merthyr Tydfil (01685-386868) and Phil will collect us at the airport and drop us of at the hotel sorted.

"Not a long drive for you this time my Scottish brother" says Phil, "are you up for this trip?" "Off course pal, looking forward to it" I reply. I pick up Ken then drive to Edinburgh airport, book in for our flight, then go for a beer. After we land, we are met by Phil who, as usual, is happy to see us. We blether all the way to the hotel which is very nice. Phil says, "Yes, the welsh ex boxers have arranged this for you both." We head down to the bar for a beer and something to eat. I explain to Ken and Phil that an old regimental pal of mine, Rab Dundass, is looking to pop through and see me at some point tonight. We order food and Phil has this covered and as we are talking, in walks Rab. I do the introductions, then we head out to Phil's local, he stays just across the road from it, The Red Lion. I travel in Rabs car as we follow Ken and Phil. The locals are very friendly as we have been in this pub a few times over the years now. Rab has another beer then says his goodbyes, "Time I was up the road he says." "Cheers pal, say hallo to family from me ok." We don't have a late night and soon say our goodbyes to Phil and get a taxi to the hotel. We chat for about 30 minutes before its lights out and bed, but for some reason Ken is up too many times.

Next day its down for breakfast. Phil will be down to see us soon and sure enough he turns up. It's a beautiful day, so he says he will take us a wee run up to a castle which is also the local museum. It's very nice inside, as he steers us around to the boxing sports area where he proudly shows of Kens photo. Ken is truly a welsh boxing hero in his own right. We drive to see all the boxing statues which are scattered around the town, and have our photos taken but it's cold now, so Phil dives into a local outdoors shop and buys Ken a woollen hat. It looks nice I lie lol. We also take in a coffee shop that Phil uses all the time, then it's a light lunch at a nice wee bar. The gig is that night, so Phil has to leave us as he is helping to organize the nights events. "Are you two lads going to be ok till I pick you up at about 8pm" he asks? "Of course, we will pal, we will find something to do" He is no sooner out the door, than we are in another pub lol then another and another, then it's time to head back to hotel to get ready for the gig that night. On the way back we pop into one wee pub that's two minutes from our hotel.

Ken goes for a pee. The lady behind the bar says, "That's Buchanan isn't it?" "Yes, I say", so now the drinks are on the house (god I love hearing that lol). She is on her phone and the pub is now full and bouncing. Ken signs this photo then that photo and this goes on for about an hour. I now say, "Sorry but we have to go, honest, thank you for your hospitality" and we laugh all the way back to our room, only half pished. "Ken you get in shower first?" "No, I am ok honest." "No yir no, get in and hurry up, I'll run an iron over your suit and shirt then it's my turn."

When I get out of the shower Ken had let Phil in. "Jock, you're not ready yet" says Phil. Ken says, "Come on Jock hurry up", whilst laughing at me. "Prick" I say under my breath. We get a taxi to the venue, it's very nice. Phil's daughter, Rhiannon Powell, and granddaughter have a wee stall set up selling Kens prints which Phil had commissioned. Phil makes the introductions, as me and Ken sit down next to Colin jones, British, Commonwealth and European welterweight champion and Geraint

Burns supper Leven

Thomas, the organiser. Robbie Regan, who claimed world titles at two different weights was also there.

Me and Ken go steady on the beer. Its early and Ken has still to go on stage and answer questions etc. When Ken does go up to the stage, I nip into another wee bar and have a few bottles, it would be a shame not to speak to others wouldn't it? It's getting on when Phil says his daughter will give us a run back to the hotel. That's very nice Phil, thanks for that, and back at the hotel we go for a night cap.

Rhiannon stays with us for a while, I think she is enjoying the crack. Also, in attendance is one of the guests from the gig. He asks Ken some questions about his boxing career, and also takes photos. Ken is in good form, enjoying his beer, as am I. I am not driving till the following afternoon so fuck it, I am hitting the beer big time lol. Next day we are up for breakfast and wait for Phil. Once he arrives, we jump in his car and drive back to Cardiff airport which took about 30 minutes. We chat all the way. We have had a great time and been well looked after yet again by the welsh folk. Once we get back to Scotland, I drive Ken home then head back to Scone.

Burns supper Leven

Old Davy Shand, who drinks in the East dock pub, said to me one day, "Jock would you be up for saying a poem at oor burns supper in the lodge, in Leven, Fife this coming year?" "Aye, what are you looking for?" "Whatever you want, we'll look after you, if you need a room for the night etc. I can get someone to book you into the Cally, (Caledonian hotel Leven)." "Nah that's ok I'll get my sister to put me up." "Right that's braw" Davey says" I'll give you a wee bell next month to tie down arrangements." He is a great old gentleman, first thing he does when he

212

comes into the pub, is shakes everyone's hand, gives the lady's a wee kiss on the cheek and asks if you want a drink, a true gentleman. So true to his word, Davey phones my hoose. "Jock, are you still ok to do a turn at oor Burns Supper, son?" "Aye but would it be ok if Jim, Janet's man and Ken Buchanan come along?" "Aye nae bother son, my brother was already going so that's good, I will pay for Kens ticket." (Fuck not even a freebie for a sporting legend). I don't think Ken likes the Suppers too much, but it gets him away from the capital for a wee while. Janet is happy enough to put us up as she likes Ken and thinks he is very funny.

On the day, I pick up Ken about 12 midday. He was sitting in the Central bar in Leith waiting for me. "Jock ur we going away the day?" "Yes, Ken it's in your diary." "Oh, I lost that he says." We pack an overnight bag, grab his suit and head for the Kingdom of Fife. Janet gives him a big cuddle on arrival at her hoose and we drink coffee and eat a sandwich as its going to be a long night. (These nights always are). We get a taxi down to the Dock for refreshments and meet my brother who is in already. He shakes Kens hand and gets the drink in. Marshal Colman the proprietor, joins us and his son Garry has arranged for a minibus for the short journey to the venue in Leven.

We all pile into the minibus after three beers, then get into the hall find our seats and hit the bar. I can't have too much as I am saying my peace later on. It turns oot to be a good wee night and my poem go's down well. (Parcel of Rogues in a Nation, a wee dressy up number). "Are you ok Ken?" I ask." "Aye, no bad pal, would you like a beer." I tell him no because I already have a couple of beers on the table. "Aye, there mine. Your drinking the half Shandy." Lol. Unusually we both win a bottle each at the raffle, which we leave on the table for the women who served us our meal during the night. Sooner than ye can think we are back on the minibus to the pub. Long story short, we are the last to leave but we had a great night, and it was straight to bed when we got back the hoose. Next day, Janet has the breakfast all ready for us, after which we say our goodbyes and head south to the capital. Once we are back in Leith Ken throws his bag into his flat and we walk round to his local, only to be met with, "Where have you been Ken?" It's all on social media, "your missing?"

Ken is calm and says "I was at Jocks hoose. "The lassie behind the bar looks relieved and she is really happy that Ken has appeared all well and good. The staff in the Central Bar look out for Ken big time. Before ye can say two beers please, two police officers walk into the pub and start speaking to Ken. The police lassie takes me to one side and takes my details. Seemingly, the care people who bring Ken his meals etc. we're not informed of his absence and reported him missing. Ken tells the police that he telt Jim, the old lad he sits next to in pub, that he was going away for a day or two. Lol. Me, I wasn't aware Ken had to tell anyone? Ken says "Look, I am in my 70's I'll do what I want." Who could disagree? No me anyway. However, it was lesson learned on my side though.

Round 14

"Boxing is a disgrace. You can make money by hitting others to death, but at the same time you lose your human dignity!"
— Mehmet Murat ildan

2020 and that bloody Virus (COVID 19)

The coronavirus hit the whole world like no one's business. We in Scotland first started being aware of it in March 2020, did it affect me? Hell yeh. The first reported coronavirus death in Scotland was on 13 March 2020. I was put on furlough and to date 8th August, I have been on it for 20 weeks. (A furlough is a temporary leave of absence from an employee's job due to the virus outbreak, sanctioned by a government decree in order to help to prevent mass redundancies.)

The UK government paid 80% of my wages for the period of furlough. All the pubs and schools were shut and most business were closed, hopefully temporarily, but unfortunately some of them will never re-open. Food shops were still open, but customers had to wear face masks before entering the premises. Anyway, I had a message sent to me on my Facebook page that Ken had been going out during lockdown, totally unaware what all the fuss was about? He was even having folk, god only knows who, into his flat? (Which was against the lockdown rules). His local pub, the Central Bar in Leith, was closed due to the lockdown, and Ken was lost.

We have to remember that his daily routine was first, out for breakfast with one of the lads. Owen smith had organised a wee rota for some lads to go with ken, then it's into his local to collect his envelope from the bar staff, containing £20, which was his to spend for the day. Normally its half (£10) in the morning then the rest in the afternoon/evening. He would sit in the same place drinking his half Shandy talking away to the locals. He enjoyed the banter and the lassies behind the bar looked after him, going out from time to time, bringing him a sandwich etc. Sad to say, as time marched on, Ken was wandering the streets and at times forgetting where he was, or where his flat was.

Owen took the decision to get him under medical care in the Edinburgh Royal Infirmary. Poor Ken. He was confused as hell and was starting to hallucinate. Owen kindly passed on Kens ward number to me so I could phone him. On occasion's when I have phoned to speak to Ken, the nurse would say, "Oh Kens just sitting here." I could hear ken asking the nurse, who was on the phone? Its Jock from Perth she would say and Ken replying, "Naw I dinnae ken him." So, I never got to speak to him. It's heart breaking. On other occasions he is ok, speaking away. Once I spoke to him and he was whispering. "Jock, I am on a train and we are all tied up There is people taking our money? Right got tae go, I hear someone coming." Then the phone goes dead. Yes, it could be the medication I suppose. Owen, who is the main stay of looking after Ken during this pandemic, has had many meetings with the doctors, care advisors etc.

2020 and that bloody Virus (COVID 19)

They have all decided Ken needs to go into a local care home, at Albert Street, Leith. I believe it is now the right Decision. He can't look after himself anymore. He is now in the Victoria Manor, which is a friendly care home, offering nursing and nursing memory care for those living with dementia. As Owen has the power of attorney for Ken, he had to phone the home to say it was ok for me to visit Ken, i.e. I am not the media etc.

As Ken is a new resident, he has to go into 14 days quarantine, before he can have any visitors. Even then it must be by appointment only and in the homes garden, in full PPE, etc., which I fully understand. As I type away, I am waiting for his 14 days period to be up, so that I can then arrange a visit, poor bugger. Our visit down to Cardiff, Wales, this September for the Ex British Boxers hall of fame is cancelled due to the virus. Maybe we will get down next year? Ken excels in the boxing environment, so another visit or two might do him the world of good. God, I hope so? So, I have booked a visit to go and see Ken at his new care home. It's during the week, at a time that suits us both, i.e. 11am at the home. This means I miss the early morning rush, I can spend 30 minutes or more with Ken and then he is ready for his lunch, at 12 o'clock. For some reason, I feel very nervous for this visit.

So, on Wednesday 19th August 2020, I get up at 7:30 pm and take the dug oot for a quick pee. Then it's back in to make us breakfast, me coffee and cereal, the wee dug, Buddy, gets toast and butter (spoiled wee shit lol). A quick wash, then it's out the door for 8:30am and get petrol? Eh, nope, the bloody que is massive lol.

Fuck it, there will be enough in the tank to get me there? I headed off early as I am not sure what is ahead off me, road works etc., because they are all over the place just now. I am lucky, I get to the care home in good time. It's a braw day, so that's good for my visit which is in the homes garden. I am a wee bit early, so I sit ootside reading the paper. Approx. five minutes later a care worker comes out and says, in a broad southern Irish accent, "Excuse me, are you Jock? "Yes" I say. "Well Ken is having a coffee and is ready for your visit now."? "Ok, sure thanks." "You will have to be in full PPE" she says. "Aye nae bother" I reply. So, I take a seat in the garden, under a gazebo and wait. Just then, out pops the man. "Hi Jock" he says. At least he recognises me I think to myself. "Hi pal how's you." "Good" he says holding his mug of coffee, "Jock do you want a cup" ken asks. "No yir fine pal. We sit down and catch up on life. The senior carer was good enough to come out and put their guest password into my IPAD, so that I could facetime Phil Jones for a wee minute. The signal wasn't great, but I think Phil was just happy to hear that his old pal was ok and looking good.

During our 30-minute chat, I asked Ken if he wouldn't mind signing a glove for me? It's for a big fan up in Aberdeenshire, by the name off John Boyce. John actually travels to Manila regularly to stay over for a while and have Manny Pacquiao sign stuff for him. Manny Pacquiao is the only eight-division world champion in the history of boxing and winner of twelve major world titles. Straight away Ken goes into his Victor Meldrew impersonation, saying the 'I don't believe it!' catchphrase, lol. "Aye nae bother pal, it wouldn't be a visit without you getting a couple of signatures Ken says and laughs to himself.

Lol that's very true. During the visit Ken says he is cold? So, one of the carers puts a wee blanked around him. The time fly's bye and my 30 minutes are over. However, I have already asked to come back for a visit and the senior carer told me that would be fine. "No problem jock, just give me a bell and we can arrange another visit when you're ready." Ken gives me a fist pump to say goodbye. Normally it's a big bear hug, but as Bob Dylan said "The times, they are a changing. I say goodbye to Ken and head back to Perth with a big smile on my face. I can't wait for next visit I am thinking, as Neil diamond blares out of the CD. I just wish my singing companion was with me?

"Ken, I'll remember for you,"
Jock.

They speak of my drinking. A Poem

Alcohol is the most widely used drug in the world. Alcohol can feel like a stimulant, for a while but it's actually a depressant. That's not to say that it makes you depressed, a fact which we are all led to believe, but it slows down your central nervous system. It stops the release of neurotransmitters in the brain which has the effect of slowing down normal bodily responses. Alcohol can also affect your mood and your mental health. Excessive intake of alcohol can have a damaging effect on normal bodily functions leading to, amongst other symptoms, high blood pressure, irregular heartbeat, liver cirrhosis, mental health impairment and even cancer. The vast majority of us like a drink, me probably one too many on occasion but we never think of the potential harm caused by that consumption. For all my years Alcohol consumption was an accepted norm within the social environment. We all liked a drink.

Here's a wee poem I found that is a wee funny 'ode to drink'. Not that I am justifying the need for a wee pint or two by the way.

They speak of my drinking. But, never of my thirst.
(3 February 2008 by Ringside)

They speak of my drinking
But, never of my thirst.
An empty glass I'm thinking
Is to be truly cursed.

They speak of my drinking. A Poem

I'd like to raise my glass
To the bouncer man
That kicks my ass
Anytime that he can

So, blacken my eye
And bloody my lip.
I'll drink the bar dry.
I'll drink every sip.

With a lass, on my right
In my left there's a beer.
I shall promise a fight
If ye look at me queer.

Pour me another shot
I shall dance without guilt.
I may show what this Scotsman
Wears under his kilt.

A fair maiden just gave me a wink.
Pour a shot of Jameson Red.
With a toast, our glasses may clink.
Alas, we go home to ma bed.

In the morning fog of dawn

They speak of my drinking. A Poem

I awake with a fright!
For it was a leprechaun
that had just spent the night!

https://allpoetry.com/Ringside.

The Menzingers are an American punk rock band from Scranton, Pennsylvania, formed in 2006. They wrote a wee song about their thirst for the bevvy and titled it. Check it out on the Internet:

They Speak of My Drinking, But Never of My Thirst.
(The Menzingers)

Round 15 🥊

"Mental health has got to be the biggest battle I've ever fought, more so than any opponent."- Tyson Fury

My Pal Ken Buchanan MBE

I don't have hundreds of photos of Ken and me together, but what I do have are thousands of happy memories. Aye, for all the time I have been honoured to know Ken I thought he had one fault, his generosity. He could never ever say no. If he had a pound in his pocket you would get 50p of it and he would even give you the shirt of his back. Yes, he enjoyed a wee drink, but people forget he gave up his youth and teenage years to dedicate himself to his dream, to become the World Boxing Champion and not many people can say they achieved their Dream in life, Ken did.

My twin sister Janet once said to me, "I can see a lot of oor dad in Ken" and she was probably right. They both boxed, both enjoyed a drink, both enjoyed life to the full and loved their families. Ken is a very proud man, especially when he talks about his family, Mark and Raymond his sons and Karen, his daughter. He would always stand tall and tell anyone who would listen, it was his dad, Tommy, who made him the boxing legend he finally became. We must all remember that its memories that are the real trophies in life, not possessions. I am very proud and honoured to call Ken a good close pal. Will we ever see his like again, I think not.

My Pal Ken Buchanan MBE

Ken Buchanan retired with a record of 61 wins 8 losses in 69 professional bouts, with 27 wins by a knockout. In the year 2000, he was elected in to the International & World Boxing Hall of Fame. He is the holder of five championship belts, the only British fighter in Boxing history ever to achieve that honour.

Kens Boxing Statistics
Name: Ken Buchanan
Born: 1945-06-28
Birthplace: Edinburgh, Scotland
Nationality: Scottish
Hometown: Edinburgh, Scotland, United Kingdom
Boxing Career: 1965 - 1982
Boxing Stance: Orthodox
Height: 5' 7½" / 171cm
Reach: 70" / 178cm
Professional Bouts: 69
Won 61 (KO 27) + lost 8 (KO 1)
Rounds boxed 555 KO% 39.13
Manager: Eddie Thomas
Trainer: Gil Clancy
Undisputed Lightweight Champion of the World 1970 – 1972.
Undefeated British & European Lightweight Champion.
Edward J. Neil Trophy '1970 American Fighter of the Year'
Inducted into the International & World Boxing Hall of Fame(s) 2000

My Pal Ken Buchanan MBE

My Family has been associated with the Buchanan family for a good number of years; from my mum, Nancy, working with Kens mum, Cathy, in Edinburgh, to my dad-boxing Ken on a number of occasions, to me almost poisoning him at a games night lol

Ken Buchanan is the biggest kindest, hearted man you would ever likely to meet. We have had some great laughs together and seen and met some of the biggest names in the world of boxing, all who spoke very highly of our nations sporting legend. This book is about two pals who both enjoy a pint on a Saturday night and who don't take life to seriously.

I am lucky, I have a lot of good memories of Ken, but as I have said somewhere in the book already, he will be remembered more when he is no longer with us. When the time comes, a lot of celebrities, footballers, boxers, etc. will all want to be seen in attendance and try to take a cord, looking good for the media. They will all talk highly of Ken, and so they should, but where were they when Ken was in hospital, at The Carseview Centre, Dundee Royal, Edinburgh Hospital, Morningside Place, Penumbra Milestone, Oxgangs Edinburgh? It's not good wishes etc. that makes you a legend it's your actions.

When you get time, you should read the interview by Aidan Smith from The Scotsman newspaper on 15th December 2012. I sat with Ken through this along with one of his old flames, Carol Ann, at her flat in Leith, Edinburgh. It has lines like "Ken Buchanan has eight envelopes to his name, all of them bursting with the dramas of his life, in and out of the boxing ring, " It finishes with the line: "If Edinburgh doesn't want him, New York will take him and cherish him."

About the Author

"Sometimes there's no way to get the upper hand without taking a few uppercuts."- Curtis Tyrone Jones

About Me, the Author

I am Jock Mcinnes MBE, MinstF

I am from a wee village called Methil, in Fife, Scotland, where many of my family still remain. I have been married for many, many years to my lovely wife Christine and we have one son, Stuart, who I really admire. All dads would say this, but he has not brought one bit of trouble to our door. Both him and his hard-working wife, Moira, have given us two beautiful grandchildren, Eilidh and Callum and we are very proud grandparents. (Bike lol it's a grandad joke?) And I can't leave out Buddy the family dog an English Cocker Spaniel. Eilidh will no doubt say, is her dog and yes, she did get him for her 11th birthday, but she kens that he is the family dug.

I am ex-forces, having served in the Black watch (RHR), as an advanced adventure training and physical training instructor. I served for 22years finishing up as a Senior non-commissioned officer (Sergeant). I also worked with the justice sector for a good number of years on the electronic tagging of offender's scheme. Why did I join the forces, well

About Me, the Author

my big brother Willie (a great soldier) had joined the year before me and our dad served for a number of years in the same Regiment. In fact, down the many years our family and the wives have had a strong connection with the Black watch, but to tell the truth the pits (Coal mines) were all closing, the brick works had gone, and employment was at a long time low, so there were fewer and fewer employment opportunities.

In sport, I was the army individual boxing champion, and the combined services runner-up. I was also the midland district Dundee/Fife boxing champion twice and represented Scotland on a number of occasions. To this day I keep in contact with my good army pal, Paddy (Derrick) Riley, who served in the Army with me in the early 70's. He was one hell of a good boxer, and currently runs the local Perth boxing club, Fair city ABC.

One of the first things I did since leaving the forces was to successfully create and managed my own Perth charity abseil team which believe it or not ran for over 15 years. It brought in thousand's off pounds for local and national charities, But I wasn't alone though, I had been ably assisted by both Mike Scott, and Peter Cruickshanks (RIP), both great lads. I Love organising challenges in my spare time and enjoy a laugh and the odd pint or two.

In my time, I have also organised and administrated several charity challenge's including, Tandem Skydiving, Mount Kinabalu, The Sahara Desert, Mount Kilimanjaro, Mount Elbrus, The Gobi Desert, Mount Toubkal, Nepal experience, Mont Etna, a fire walk, and the climb to the summit of Moldoveanu.

During my fundraising years, I have raised well over two million pounds for local and national charities and was awarded an MBE for

About Me, the Author

services to charity from her majesty the Queen. Am I finished trekking and raising money for others? Nah 60+ years old now and I will still be doing it at 73 lol.

You can contact me via my website at https://jockmcinnes.co.uk

229

Scottish Colloquial Words used within this book

Scottish Word - Meaning

Aboot -	About
Aff -	Off
Bletherin -	Talking
Bouk –	Feeling sick
Breeks -	Trousers
Cannae –	Can't
Druth -	Thirst due to excessive alcohol drinking
Dinnae -	Don't
Doon -	Down
Fitbaw -	Football
Gid -	Good
Hallo-	Hello
Hame -	Home
Hen-	Lady, girl
Hoose -	House
Hud –	Had or Hold
Huv -	Have
Huvnay –	Haven't
Jammys -	Pyjamas
Ken-	Know (When it's not a person's name)

Scottish Word - Meaning

Scottish Word	Meaning
Nae -	No
Naw -	No
Oor -	Our
Oot -	Out
Pished -	Drunk
Pishing doon -	Raining heavily
Sair -	Sore
Swally –	Drink alcohol
Tae -	Too
Telt -	Told
Whits –	What's
Wi -	With
Wissnae –	Wasn't
Widdnae -	Wouldn't
Wrang -	Wrong
Ya -	You
Yeh -	Yes
Yi -	You
Yip -	Yes
Yir –	You're
Yirsel -	Yourself
Yis –	You people
Yiv –	You have

Index

Index

Index

Index

Index

Index

Index

Index

Index

CPSIA information can be obtained
at www.ICGtesting.com
Printed in the USA
BVHW041358131020
590913BV00012BA/208